Making Choice Theory Work in A QUALITY CLASSROOM

Sally Berman

SkyLight
TRAINING AND PUBLISHING, INC.
Arlington Heights, Illinois

Making Choice Theory Work in the Quality Classroom
Published by IRI/SkyLight Training and Publishing, Inc.
2626 S. Clearbrook Dr., Arlington Heights, IL 60005
800-348-4474 or 847-290-6600
FAX 847-290-6609
info@iriskylight.com
http://www.iriskylight.com

Creative Director: Robin Fogarty
Managing Editor: Barbara Harold
Editor: Sabine Vorkoeper
Graphic Designers: Bruce Leckie, Heidi Ray
Cover and Illustration Designer: David Stockman
Formatter: Heidi Ray
Production Supervisor: Bob Crump

ISBN 1-57517-040-X

2086-8-97McN
Item Number 1525
06 05 04 03 02 01 00 99 98 97   15 14 13 12 11 10 9 8 7 6 5 4 3 2 1

Dedication

To my chosen partner and best friend, Al,
and the Tennessee teachers whose comments
intiated the thinking that resulted in this book.

Acknowledgments

During an early session of a graduate course I taught in Nashville, Tennessee, in June 1996, I described just how I would manage the class to the participants. I told them that I expected us to have different pictures of how a class worked best. I told them that my goal was to help them master the content, have fun, and transfer learning back to their own classrooms while I managed the class in the way described in this book. At the end of the class, after forty-plus contact hours, some of the participants came to me and said, "We heard you explain at the beginning of the course how you were going to do things, but we didn't see how it was going to work, and we were a little bit uneasy. We decided to give your style a chance to see if it would work. We are pleasantly amazed to tell you that it does. We are still not really sure how you did it—we just know that we did have fun and we did learn—we are amazed by how much we learned."

When I taught a quality classroom course for New York State United Teachers in August of the same year, the participants asked for more information about choice theory and multiple intelligences theory and how they fit into the quality classroom picture. I decided to sketch that picture by writing this book. It is meant to show how cooperative learning, multiple intelligences, authentic assessment/evaluation, quality school, choice theory, systems thinking, and lead management integrate to create a quality classroom. When all of these puzzle pieces fit together they form a picture of a high-energy, warm, caring, student-centered place of learning where the teacher facilitates and mediates and everyone constantly looks for ways to improve.

Until the Nashville people gave me their parting comment and the New York people asked for better information, I had not realized just how many concepts I had woven together to develop my classroom management style. I thank these participants for helping me improve my picture of what I do when I teach. I believe that the classroom practices described in this book will work for learners of any age. The Nashville and New York people co-verified that belief this past summer.

I thank my husband, Al, for giving up e-mail time so that I could write, for providing hot coffee and ice water on demand, for encouraging and loving me, and for always being there. I am indebted to our two Siberian huskies, Murphy and Mike (both girls), who helped me pace myself. When they knew that I needed to write longer, Mike lay behind my chair so that I couldn't get up without a struggle while Murphy lay on my feet. Murphy let me know when it was break time by bouncing off me and the chair, making it impossible to keep my hands on the keyboard.

I thank Robin Fogarty at IRI/SkyLight, who encouraged me to get a manuscript to her and suggested the T-charts at the beginning of each chapter. I thank Carolyn Chapman, whose multiple intelligences work for IRI/SkyLight whetted my curiosity about Howard Gardner's theory.

I thank Jeanette McDaniel, who taught the Glasser Institute intensive weeks in which I participated; Diane Gossen, who taught me through the final certification week and whose writings have clarified my thinking about classroom management; and Dr. Glasser, for choice theory and his picture of a quality school.

I thank Lake Superior, which is the perfect landscape for me to gaze upon when I am groping for the next phrase or clarifying the last one, and the clear northern air and light that help me incubate thoughts as I walk.

Thanks to everyone and every place that helped me write this book. I hope it helps each reader create a joyous quality classroom.

Contents

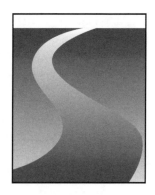

Introduction

I have had at least four "careers" as a public high school teacher. I began my career with a good understanding of my content area, an almost crusading desire to help students learn that content, and some pretty ineffective ideas about classroom management. My principal, department chairman, and mentor-teacher gave me lots of ideas and suggestions about how to be a more effective classroom leader, and I tried out most of them. What I finally realized was that I was not them and that I needed to find a blend of their suggestions and my own ideas that would become my personal management style.

I really dedicated myself to "controlling" the classroom because I *knew* that I could get kids to learn if I could only get them to settle down and listen to me. After about three years of experimenting with and evaluating leadership strategies, I developed a style that I now think of as the *coercive guilting buddy*. A coercive guilting buddy says: "I really like teaching you kids and I know that you like learning from me. I know that you'll do what I ask because you like me a lot and you like what you're learning from me, so just play along with what I ask you to do and follow the rules. If you don't, I'll hurt you, and I'll use the silent treatment to let you know that you hurt me." That final sentence was rarely spoken; it hung between us as an understanding and a threat.

I now believe that the coercive buddy system worked for me because my classes were made up of highly motivated students who were convinced that doing well in high school chemistry would help them get into the best colleges and universities and become successful doctors, dentists, engineers, and scientists. I also had strong support from their parents. Most of my students during those first years were going into science, engineering, or medicine after they graduated from high school. They came from stable, two-parent families in which, for the most part, dad went to work every morning, mom stayed home, and both parents expected their children to be successful in school. The quality worlds of those students included very strong pictures of school success and of their parents, so they did pretty much as I asked.

I used the coercive guilting buddy leadership style for about two years. Although I believed that it worked reasonably well, I never felt physically comfortable with the guilting behaviors I was using. After tinkering with my leadership style, it evolved into the *buddy monitor.* The buddy monitor says: "I will tell you the classroom rules and the reasons for those rules. I am the adult with the experience, so I know what the rules should be. I will also tell you the consequences for breaking the rules. If you break a rule, expect me to know it and expect to suffer the consequence. If you disagree with the consequence, I will ask you to discuss your disagreement with a disciplinarian. I know you won't break the rules because they are reasonable and because you like me and this class so much. You can follow the rules for me, can't you?"

Most of my students still had schoolwork and their parents as strong quality world pictures, so I still had good "control" in the classroom. I still saw myself as a strong motivator and dispenser of knowledge. I felt more physically comfortable with this leadership style, which my body said was a less confrontational, emotional, and angry way to lead the classroom. I had very few "discipline problems." My students were academically successful. I gained a reputation among the administrators and guidance counselors as a teacher who could be successful with problem kids—kids whose academic or social skills needed strengthening or kids who used disruptive behaviors in other classes.

I now believe that I was successful with those kids because I explained the reasons for the classroom rules and did not use anger as a control tool. I believe that the behaviors I chose to use empowered the difficult kids and helped me become part of their quality worlds. However, I didn't analyze my success in those terms at the time—I just enjoyed it and coasted. I fine-tuned my management style and made no major changes for about fifteen years.

Then I discovered cooperative learning. I had tried group work on and off over the years, and had always believed that kids could learn from each other. However, I had reservations because I knew that when I let kids work in groups, they always chose to work with their buddies. In addition, some kids always worked alone because no one else chose to work with them.

The cooperative learning model developed by Johnson and Johnson gave me the tools and rationale for assigning kids to groups, for keeping the groups heterogeneous, and for teaching social skills that would help groups function more effectively in an academic setting. I especially appreciated the emphasis on social skills.

The demographics of my school had changed over the years. We now had significant numbers of students who lived in subsidized housing—students whose parents had moved them to the suburbs to get them out of city gangs. We had large numbers of non-native English speakers, some of whom understood almost no English. Students with learning disabilities and behavior "problems" were being included in average classrooms. Forty percent of the "regular" kids came from nontraditional families—single parent or second-marriage or partner families. Kids from two-parent families rarely had a parent at home full-time. Many kids returned to empty homes after school. And many of them did not include pictures of school-work and/or home in their quality worlds.

I wanted a structure that would help my classroom become a model of inclusion and a place where students wanted to succeed and were willing to work to be successful. I didn't say it this way; I now know that I wanted my classroom to become a picture in the quality worlds of the kids. Cooperative learning helped. I also discovered that I had changed my leadership style. I did not change intentionally, and it took several months before I noticed the effects of using cooperative learning. My leadership style had become that of a *monitor-manager,* with a bit of leftover buddy monitoring and a dollop of coercion.

The monitor-manager says: "I'll tell you the classroom rules and the reasons for those rules. I am the adult with the experience, so I know what the rules should be. I will ask you to evaluate your behavior, what your classroom performance strengths are, and what performance areas you want to improve."

I tried to coerce students to use successful cooperative behaviors by bribing them with bonus grades and praise. The classroom did become more student centered and learner driven. I no longer thought of it as "my" classroom; it was "our" classroom. I felt physically comfortable explaining new concepts, explaining the structure of a cooperative activity, and monitoring student teamwork. Most of the time I was the guide on the side. I felt twinges of physical discomfort when I awarded bonuses or used praise, but I told myself that this was a small price to pay for student compliance to the rules of cooperative groups. I was thrilled as student performance improved. Cooperative learning seemed to be a tool that helped students improve test scores, thinking skills, and behaviors.

Finally, I learned about choice (control) theory as presented by Dr. William Glasser. I chose to believe what choice theory says about internal motivation for behavior because this belief helped me understand why traditional classroom management styles and methods of discipline did not work. I read the powerful argument that Alfie Kohn presents for the coercive nature of rewards, and Diane Gossen's insightful ideas about classroom and school management. I studied W. Edwards Deming's ideas about quality management and its effect on productivity and morale in the workplace.

To the best of my ability, I became a classroom *manager.* The classroom manager says: "Together we will develop classroom rules and the reasons for those rules. I may ask you to include some rules that you may not have thought of by yourselves. I will explain the reasons for those rules, which will have something to do with your physical or emotional safety or the rules (laws) of the school. I will ask you to evaluate your behavior and learning and identify your classroom performance strengths, what areas you want to strengthen, what specific plans you have to achieve that, and how you want to celebrate success." I stopped bribing kids for using cooperative behaviors just because I asked for those behaviors. Instead, I asked kids to self-evaluate the effectiveness of their teamwork and learning when they used the targeted behaviors. I saw how self-evaluation promoted stronger internal motivation and more rapid improvement better than all of the bribes I had offered.

The classroom was truly ours. It was *us*-centered. Students now included pictures of working in this classroom into their quality worlds, and the results were improved teamwork, content learning, thinking skills, and internal motivation. I still buddied—a little. I still rewarded—after the fact and as a personal celebration. And I discovered that this we-centered, interactive, collegial classroom worked well for learners of all ages, from the little ones to the adults.

What follows is my model for "quality driving" in a quality classroom. I hope that other teachers will find parts or all of the model helpful as they work toward quality in their own classrooms.

Using This Book

This book is about integrating systems thinking, quality management practices, applied choice theory, cooperative learning, targeted multiple intelligences, and authentic assessment to create effective

IRI/SkyLight Training and Publishing, Inc.

classroom leadership. The driving analogy that I used to introduce each chapter evolved from the car analogy that Dr. William Glasser has used in explaining such choice theory concepts as total behavior and basic needs. Readers can find a brief explanation and graphic of this car in Chapter 4. I encourage readers to begin using this book by going through all of the driving pieces before exploring the rest of the book to develop the picture that a complex activity (like classroom management or successful car ownership and use) involves integrating many different behaviors and knowledge bases.

Next, I ask readers to examine the introduction, think about its description of the different classroom management styles that I used, and identify their own classroom styles. If they are "not yet" classroom *managers,* I ask them to write themselves a note answering these questions: Does your management style work because coercion works? Because your students genuinely like you and will do as you ask because they want to be loving and giving with you? Because your students love their caregivers who value success in school? Because your students want to be free from the hassle of the discipline office with its consequences? Or because using acceptable behavior in your classroom gives your students academic survival? Do you have kids who just will not buy into your classroom and will not "respond" to your management style? What do you think they want when their behavior does not match your definition of acceptable behavior? How could you find out what they want? Do you really know what is going on with "the kid who," or have you been making assumptions about him or her?

Next, I encourage readers to browse through the book, looking at the T-charts that introduce each chapter and the section headings. The T-charts describe what a teacher and classroom look and sound like when the teacher integrates the chapter concepts into his or her management style. The section headings identify the knowledge base components for each main concept and my personal applications of that knowledge base. Section headings that identify ideas are generally nouns, and headings for application sections tend to start with verbs. Each chapter includes at least one activity that I encourage the readers to use in their own classrooms as they develop their quality management skills. I hope that readers will also use tools like journals and rubrics, and strategies like concurrent and self-evaluation as they help their students become quality learners. I encourage readers to adapt some of my classroom techniques for their own use and to keep a personal journal in which they record what they did, their reason(s) for choosing those behaviors, how well the behaviors worked, and what they want to change or improve the next time they use similar behaviors.

I wrote this book to be a companion to *A Multiple Intelligences Road to a Quality Classroom.* In that book, I describe activities that teachers can do with their students to help the students become quality learners. Teachers who use that book find that those activities use about ten percent of their classroom time. This piece describes what teachers can do the other ninety percent of the time to eliminate fear and coercion, model learning tasks, honor all ways of being intelligent, collect authentic information about student learning, and make their classrooms joyful places to work and learn. Teachers who practice this integrated model of classroom management will develop classrooms that are true learning communities.

IRI/SkyLight Training and Publishing, Inc.

CHAPTER

1

Shifting Gears

Changing the System

An educational adage I have heard for years is that teachers teach as they were taught, and that their classroom management starts out somewhat shaky, improves over the course of three to five years, peaks after about seven years, and then plateaus for the rest of their careers. This, to me, is like saying that when we learn to drive we start out in neutral, take some time to learn the difference between shifting into reverse and first gear, finally get the car into first, and never shift into a different gear. Would anyone choose to drive a car like that? Wouldn't it take forever to get where we wanted to go if we were permanently stuck in first gear? Do we want to shift into a higher gear in classroom management? I believe the "classroom car" will get students on their way to better learning in less time if we just "shift up" our management.

CHANGING THE SYSTEM

Looks Like	Sounds Like
• reading books by Senge, Kohn, Glasser, Good, Gossen, IRI/SkyLight authors	• "I've read about this—I wonder if it will work with our kids."
• multiple intelligences in use	• lots of "learning noise"
• authentic assessment in use	• "This time we'll assess by . . . ."
• teacher facilitating and mediating	• "Did you think about trying . . . ? I don't know? What do you think?"

Figure 1.1

Whenever I thought about creating a quality classroom, I would say to myself, ". . . the problem is that Deming and Glasser say that to get quality we need to change the system, and I just can't change the system all by myself. If *the rest of the school and the district administration* don't want to change the system, I can't do much about it." Then I had a new perception. The classroom I managed was its own microsystem. This new perception helped free up my thinking and let me find new ways of looking at changing the system in ways that would help my students. Maybe I didn't have the power to change the macrosystem, the entire school, but as manager, I did have the power to change the system of one classroom.

Defining the Old System

The first thing I wanted to do was to define the system I was trying to change. I thought that describing it would help me clarify what changes I wanted to make and how those changes might fit together.

Here's my picture of the old system. It is an example of what Peter Senge calls a *balancing feedback* system (see Figure 1.2).

A balancing feedback system tends to maintain the status quo. The system that I wanted to change certainly does that. Teachers

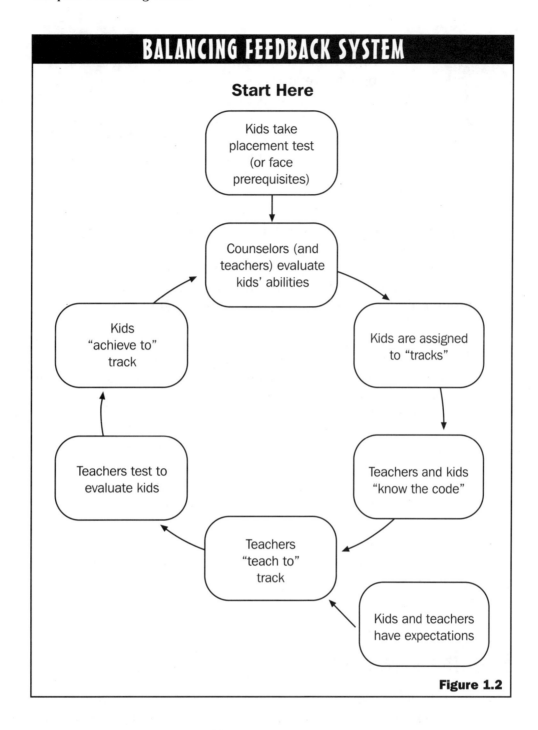

BALANCING FEEDBACK SYSTEM

Start Here

Kids take placement test (or face prerequisites)

Counselors (and teachers) evaluate kids' abilities

Kids are assigned to "tracks"

Teachers and kids "know the code"

Kids and teachers have expectations

Teachers "teach to" track

Teachers test to evaluate kids

Kids "achieve to" track

Figure 1.2

expect the results that the assigned track predicts, the kids know their placement tracks and expect to achieve at those levels, and the teaching and learning (or achievement) combine to verify the placement. "They're only average!" or "They're the gifted and talented group!" become self-fulfilling prophecies. I believe that the system described by this feedback loop gives teachers, kids, and counselors what they expected to get when the placement was first made.

1. Tell the class that this is an individual activity. Say, "I want you to do a graphic of green. Let me give you a few examples. To do a graphic of green, I can *(fitting actions to words—doing the graphic on chart paper in green marker or on the chalk board in green chalk)* draw a leaf or I can draw a string bean. Now you take a couple of minutes to do an individual graphic of green."

2. Give students a few moments to do the graphic. Then say, "I would like to know what graphics of green you did." Ask for volunteers to share their graphics with the class, or call on students at random and ask them to share their answers with the class. Make lavish positive comments about the pictured green objects. Include the names of the objects as part of the praise.

3. Then say, "Now I want you to do a graphic of yellow. Do an individual graphic." Ask the students if they want you to provide an example or two. Give students a few moments to do the individual work.

4. Again, ask students to volunteer to share their graphics with the rest of the class, or call on randomly selected students to do the sharing. The graphics of yellow will all be yellow objects. This is an example of a balancing feedback loop. Through the examples shown and the praise given, you indirectly tell kids that the graphic is the picture of an object. You will get what you expect because the students want to give the "right" answers. ◆

Creating a New System

After defining the existing system, I asked myself what I could do to create a *reinforcing feedback* system to replace the old one. A reinforcing feedback system would help students learn more, remember their learning better, and experience greater success in the classroom. Based on what I had learned about choice theory, I decided that the key to the new system was self-evaluation. I believed that the best way to find out what students already knew was to ask them; the best way to find out whether or not students had effective learning behaviors, such as good questioning skills, persistence, effective use of study time, good reading comprehension, and the ability to accurately identify where they needed help, was to ask them. I would tell them that their self-evaluation would be private and personal unless they wanted to share it with me. I told them that the key to developing new, more successful learning behaviors was to honestly evaluate the behaviors they were using and then find new behaviors to replace old ones that were not working. I told them that their content learning would be concurrently evaluated—that they would show me and tell me what they had learned and share their learnings with classmates. I helped by managing the classroom, explaining and clarifying new content learning, structuring learning activities that included the demonstration of learning in a variety of ways, asking everyone in the class to be willing to take a chance by working outside of their own comfort zones from time to time, and, in doing so, give everyone a chance to work inside their own comfort zones.

Gardner's theory of multiple intelligences is discussed later in the book; but for now I want to say that I believe that many students do not do well in school because they are expected to work in verbal/linguistic or logical/mathematical ways when they are more comfortable working in musical/rhythmic, bodily/kinesthetic, visual/spatial, or naturalistic ways. I also believe that many students have not been given opportunities to develop their intrapersonal/introspective skills, so they do not know which of their learning behaviors are helpful and which are not. Students who are not aware of which behaviors are not working are doomed to repeat the same ineffective learning patterns over and over again.

I mulled over all of these ideas and created the reinforcing feedback system (see Figure 1.3).

Putting the New System to Work

I put the new system in place. Initially the kids were very uncomfortable self-evaluating. I helped by suggesting some very structured ways to examine behaviors and some very specific behaviors to examine. I also repeated over and over that I was not interested in blame or excuses—I just wanted them to honestly decide how effective their behaviors were. Guided practice helped them organize self-evaluation as an effective behavior. I did not criticize personal learning plans. I let them evaluate the effectiveness of their learning plans by looking at the results.

As they became more skillful in self-evaluation, they also became more successful in learning new behaviors from each other and crafting more effective learning plans.

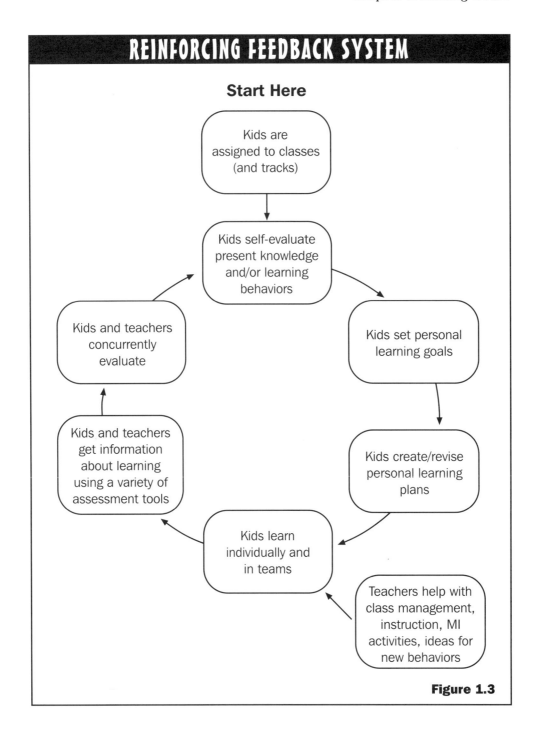

REINFORCING FEEDBACK SYSTEM

Start Here

Kids are assigned to classes (and tracks)

Kids self-evaluate present knowledge and/or learning behaviors

Kids set personal learning goals

Kids create/revise personal learning plans

Teachers help with class management, instruction, MI activities, ideas for new behaviors

Kids learn individually and in teams

Kids and teachers get information about learning using a variety of assessment tools

Kids and teachers concurrently evaluate

Figure 1.3

The kids were also uncomfortable with concurrent evaluation the first time we tried it. (It's a process in which they would demonstrate their knowledge and learning in a face-to-face session with me or a classmate.) But they soon said that they preferred it to traditional testing because they could use the new system to give me a better, more complete picture of what they knew. Kids accepted responsibility for their own achievement and behaviors.

I decided that this loop did provide a reinforcing feedback system. We were not maintaining the status quo; we were increasing learning effectiveness, achievement, and responsible behavior every time we went around the loop. We were improving the quality of learning and the products that demonstrated the learning every time we went around the loop. The microsystem that I managed had become more kid friendly.

1. Do a think/pair/share. Ask kids to think and visualize individually about this instruction: Think blue. Ask kids to think of at least three individual answers in five to ten seconds. Tell them when it is time to choose a partner and share answers with the partner. Ask partners to list all of their answers that are different. Ask them to do the list in words and as a graphic. Give pairs five minutes to do the list.

2. Ask pairs to volunteer to share their list with the rest of the class, or randomly call on pairs. When a pair has shared its list with the class, say "Thank you." Do not praise answers. Spend the same amount of time acknowledging different answers.

3. After several pairs have shared their lists with the class, ask "Did all of you have blue objects on your lists? Did any pair have a swatch of blue—just the color blue? Did any pair have the word blue? If you had the word blue, did you write it in blue or in some other color? Did anyone picture an unhappy person— a person who is "blue"? Is there a right way to think blue, or would any of these be correct ways to think blue?"

4. Ask pairs to self-evaluate. Ask them what they learned about the different ways that people visualize. Ask them how this learning could change their own thinking the next time the class does a think/pair/share. Ask them what they did to help each other and what they would like to do differently the next time the class does a think/pair/share. Ask one of the partners in each pair to record the answers to the self-evaluation questions.

5. A few days later, do another think/pair/share. This time, tell kids to think purple. After the pairs do their lists and share them with the class, ask them to do another self-evaluation. Ask them to focus on the quality of their individual thinking and

their teamwork. What was different from "Think blue"? Were the differences improvements or just differences?

6. As pairs share their lists with the class, you will probably see more divergent thinking and creativity in the answers. This activity is an example of reinforcing feedback. The instructions, teacher feedback, and self-evaluation all emphasize the idea that it's all right for different individuals to possess different ways of thinking. No one way of visualizing a color is better than any other. ◆

A postscript: As time passed, I came to expect the success, achievement, and learning climate that the new system encouraged. I took these positives for granted or even, I admit, wondered why we didn't progress faster. I celebrated less and less until one day, when we had a visitor. The visitor watched the kids working together; examined their work, which was displayed on the walls; went through a stack of their old work that was temporarily stored in the back of the room; and, finally, after the kids left, came to me and asked, "And what level of gifted and talented do you teach?"

I do not like to label kids, but the macrosystem labeled the kids in this class "average." I heard the question and felt my skin prickle with excitement and my breath catch with joy and pride. I thought, "That's the quality we've reached by changing the system!" I said, "The average level, and thank you for helping me remember how far they have come."

The next day I shared the incident with the kids, and we celebrated success.

CHAPTER

2

Windows Up! A.C. On!

Managing the Climate

For most of us, the days of driving around in a car that has a physically uncomfortable climate are a thing of the past. But I still remember the days when I told people my car had 450 air conditioning—I lowered all four windows and drove at 50 miles per hour, and sometimes I was fairly cool driving in hot summer weather. Although the wind and noise always gave me a "travel hangover," the heat in the car would have been too unbearable with the windows rolled up. I distinctly remember preferring plane or train travel because it included air conditioning. Today I cannot imagine driving in a hot car; I really appreciate a comfortable climate. Isn't the same thing true of our classrooms? Don't we need to establish and maintain a quality climate for effective teaching and learning to take place?

A QUALITY CLIMATE

Looks Like	Sounds Like
• plenty of light	• buzzing voices
• unlittered	• "I'll put that away if we're finished."
• decorated with kid stuff	• "This is our best work."
• teacher is hard to "spot"	• energetic, enthusiastic buzzing
• kids working in small groups	• rhyming, rhythmic, musical
• circles of desks	• "Let's compare ideas."
• kids moving around	• "This class is fun."

Figure 2.1

The first aspect of quality management I always attend to is establishing a climate that nurtures quality work. A quality-nurturing climate must be in place before any other management techniques can be effective. Sure I've seen some quality work come out of classrooms in which the teacher could be described as bossing rather than leading. But what made such classrooms work is that the boss teachers had established quality climates that encouraged students to do their best. The students knew that their teachers expected them to do quality work, believed that they could, and cared about them, so they did quality work.

Three separate aspects of climate work together in all classrooms to promote the highest quality work. Students need to feel physically comfortable and safe in the classroom. They need to feel emotionally safe—encouraged, trusted, liked, and accepted. Finally, they need to feel collegially safe. They need to know that each person in the classroom is expected to have her or his own individual perceptions and beliefs, that disagreements are normal and expected, that there are strengthening, respectful ways in which they can disagree, and that consensus includes space for a minority opinion.

The Physical Climate

An ideal classroom has plenty of light, both natural and artificial. Students can find bright and shaded reading corners. Room temperature is a fairly constant 70–75 degrees Fahrenheit, and the humidity is about 50 percent. The room is clean and bright, with lots of "kid art" on the walls. The room is insulated from outside noise. Unforturnately, few classrooms meet this ideal.

Teachers often feel they have little or no control over their physical environment. I once taught in a building where the ceilings were collapsing and the plaster was falling from the walls. In another building, room temperature and ventilation were poorly controlled, most rooms had no windows, and sound leaked through all of the walls. I taught a summer school class to adults in a cafeteria with dirty tables and bugs running across the floor. I have also taught in rooms with no black or white boards, no flip charts—no place to keep track of ongoing notes or brainstorming ideas.

I could have spent time complaining about the physical conditions in any of these scenarios, blamed others for the poor facilities, and used the poor physical climate to excuse a lack of quality in my teaching or the students' learning. Instead, I said to myself, "There are some physical problems here. I can wipe up dirt and organize materials so the room is at least tidy, neat, and as clean as possible. I can discuss behaviors with students so that they feel physically safe with each other—so that they know that no one will physically hurt anyone else. I can be creative with the materials and facilities that I do have. And I can tell my students that I believe in doing my best to control what I can without wasting time fretting or being angry about conditions I cannot control. I can ask students to work with me to create and maintain the best physical conditions as best we can, and to overlook the conditions we cannot control and not use them as an excuse for doing less than quality work."

I found that acting and speaking out these thoughts in the classroom helped focus all of us on what we wanted, which was to do quality work.

The Emotional Climate

A classroom with a good emotional climate feels safe, welcoming, and charged with energy. A stranger feels welcome when entering this classroom. Students must be willing to take intellectual risks in the classroom in order to do quality work. Students who feel emotionally safe are more likely to become risk takers. I work to establish a safe-risk classroom climate by modeling trusting, accepting behaviors and by encouraging students to do the same.

I believe that I can begin modeling that behavior from day one by welcoming my students with a smile and a pleasant greeting, by introducing myself, and by standing close to the door, where I'm easily accessible. When students leave class, I say goodbye, thank them for the work we did together, and tell them that I look forward to our next meeting. I try to stand near the door as they leave. These greetings and farewells take time, and I could be spending that time doing personal organizing. But spending this time on the students says to them, "I really care about you as a person. I know that you are the reason this class exists, and I am glad that you are a member."

During the first session of each class I also tell students, "I want us all to respect and accept each other in this class. I know that we will not all be 'best friends.' I do believe that we can work together in a pleasant, professional, polite way to produce quality work. In order for that to happen, we need to remember that what we *say* to someone can hurt just as much as any physically abusive action. When I talk to you, when you talk to me, and when you talk to each other, find ways to encourage and use 'put-ups,' not 'put-downs.' And please, no teasing. You may think that your friends don't mind your teasing but that may not always be the case. Can you think of a time when someone was 'only teasing' you and you didn't quite see it that way? Or maybe you just didn't feel like being teased at the time? Let's be careful about how we talk to each other—*what* we say and *how* we say it."

I also ask students to write journal entries that record their thoughts and feelings about what I just said. I begin brainstorming sessions by reminding students that we encourage each other and defer judgment about ideas. I let them know when a classroom activity is based on an idea that I learned from someone else. And I model, model, model.

I avoid the sarcastic come-backs or questions that teachers often use to disagree with students or influence their behaviors. I do not gossip about students or other teachers. I work pleasantly and professionally with other teachers. I remind myself that I am the only person I can control, and that I want to present a model of emotionally safe behavior to students. The modeling and encouraging combine to create an atmosphere of acceptance and emotional safety that promotes quality work.

IRI/SkyLight Training and Publishing, Inc.

1. This activity is done in groups of three. One member of the group is the journalist, who asks the celebrity, "What is your favorite food? What is your favorite color? What is your favorite exercise activity? What is your favorite kind of weather and what are your reasons for liking that kind of weather?" A second member of the group is the celebrity, who tells the team his or her favorite food, color, exercise activity, and type of weather. The third member of the group is the graphic artist, who sketches a silhouette of the celebrity's head on a sheet of paper and writes the answers inside the silhouette. The roles rotate in the group until each person has done each job. Students will then introduce each other to the class. Each journalist will introduce the celebrity whom he or she interviewed.

2. After all the students have been introduced, ask them to self-evaluate by answering these questions: What did I do well as a journalist or graphic artist? What did I do well as a member of my team? What do I want to improve the next time I work in a team? ◆

The Collegial Climate

People who work in a good collegial climate expect their coworkers to see the world differently from the way they do, and honor those differences. They do not expect agreement. They know that their leader/manager expects them to be able to work through their differences in an open and respectful dialogue.

As I reflect on my years in the classroom, I believe that I have always provided physical safety. (Perhaps this was partially due to my content area; chemistry teachers tend to be very aware of the need for physical safety.) My best work with emotional safety followed my implementation of Johnson and Johnson's model of cooperative learning in the classroom. However, I am just beginning to do my best work with collegial safety, which I believe is a special degree of emotional safety.

Diane Gossen's work showed me the differences between *conventional, congenial,* and *collegial* leaders. The conventional leader expects everyone to do as she says and doesn't especially care how they feel about it. The congenial leader hopes that everyone will see things her way—especially after she has explained how reasonable that way is—and wants unanimity.

The collegial leader, building on a principle of Dr. Glasser's choice theory, knows that everyone has her or his own unique perceptions and understandings. She knows that each individual has her or his own unique reality. The collegial leader does not just accept differences, she expects and welcomes them. She says to students, "I know that we will all have our own pictures of how this activity (or this course) will work best. I want us to discuss our differences, otherwise we may begin to resent each other. I also want us to understand that we will need to reach consensus about how to run this activity (or this course) so that we can move on. I want us to remember that consensus does not mean unanimity. It means that we've heard different ideas, we've given people an opportunity to contribute, and we've decided on a course of action. I expect disagreement. I will never say that you are wrong and that I am right. However, I may tell you that I do not agree with you and ask you to try doing things my way. Or I may say that I like your way better. Or we may find a way to combine our ideas to reach new insights and understandings and ways of doing things. Can we agree to talk things out so that submerged resentments don't sabotage our relationship and get in the way of quality?"

For me, this picture of collegiality roots the saying "tug at ideas, not people" in a solid understanding of human psychology. The picture sets collegiality as the keystone to emotional safety.

1. Do a think/pair/share. Ask students, "What do people say to each other when they disagree that could sound like a put-down? Think of at least three comments in the next ten seconds." After ten seconds, ask students to find a partner and compare answers. Give the pairs a couple of minutes to talk; then do a wraparound to collect all of the answers that are different.

2. Write the answers on a large sheet of chart paper. When they are all recorded, ask students, "Do we want to disagree with each other like this? Do we want classmates to feel put down, or do we want them to feel encouraged? Can we all agree not to use these comments when we disagree with each other?"

3. Use a large red marker to draw the circle/slash "banned" sign around the list of comments. Ask students to sign the list to indicate their agreement to not use the comments.

4. Then do another think/pair/share by asking students, "What can people say to each other when they disagree that might *not* sound like a put-down?" Again, suggest that each individual think of at least three comments.

5. After partners have talked, collect all of the different suggestions that students have. Then ask, "Do we want to use these comments when we disagree? Can we disagree so that classmates feel that disagreeing is O.K? Can we agree to use these new comments when we disagree?" Ask students to sign the new list to show their willingness to use these non-put-downs when they disagree.

6. Ask students to self-evaluate by completing this sentence: "Disagreeing in a way that does not put someone down is like *(my two favorite snack foods)* because both are *(three ways they are alike)* because *(reasons for the comparison)*." ◆

When I picture a quality classroom, I see a classroom that, first and foremost, has a quality climate. I believe that while a teacher may scrupulously model W. E. Deming's ideas about quality management, she will not see quality products from her students if she has not established a quality climate. Students who feel physically, emotionally, and collegially safe are working in a classroom where quality management will work. Although students who feel physically or emotionally threatened or who feel that being different is wrong *may* produce good work, they will not produce their *best* work. The classroom will not be a picture in their quality worlds. They will continue to be slightly resistant learners and the teacher will continue to feel the need to use coercion to control student behavior. A quality climate promotes trust, risk taking, acceptance of individual differences, and a willingness to work things out. Students feel encouraged to do their best work, and the teacher feels in control as she mediates and facilitates learning.

CHAPTER

3

Steering with Style

Lead Managing for Quality Classwork

I see many drivers who seem to pay little attention to their steering. Their cars wander from the center line to the white "fog line" and back. They seem to have trouble finding the center of the lane and staying there. The daughter of such a driver once told him, "Dad, if you had driven home in a straight line we would have traveled half the distance and gotten there in half the time." Do we steer our classrooms carefully? Do teaching and learning follow the direction we want them to take, or do they wander with the latest "hot topic"? How can we ensure the quality steering of our classrooms?

LEAD MANAGING FOR QUALITY CLASSWORK

Looks Like	Sounds Like
• graffiti wall of "real-world" connections to schoolwork	• "I read/heard/saw . . ."
• posters of careers related to schoolwork	• "This is important to know because . . ."
• KWL chart	• "Tell me more."
• rubrics/standards for evaluating work	• "What is a quality job?"
• teacher demonstrating the task	• "Did I show that clearly? Do I need to repeat anything?"
• students doing individual self-evaluation	• "Let me tell you what I did well."

Figure 3.1

My knowledge of lead managing a classroom to facilitate quality work is based on the ideas of Dr. William Glasser, W. Edwards Deming, David and Roger Johnson, and Diane Gossen among others (see the bibliography for source materials). Dr. Deming developed the foundation for lead management by emphasizing that low variation is the key to producing quality goods and to establishing reliability, trustworthiness, dependability, and consistency. He also insisted that genuine cooperation expands quality while competition destroys it. He taught that a management philosophy of building on good things and expecting the best of people leads to quality, while expecting the worst destroys quality. Dr. Deming's fourteen-point theory of quality management is the model on which most other quality management theories are based.

Dr. Glasser condensed Deming's model into a four-point model of lead management in schools. David and Roger Johnson developed the model of managing for cooperation that I relied on in my classroom. Diane Gossen emphasizes the need for the teacher to model the use of self-evaluation as a tool for change and growth. I have created a personal synthesis of the Deming/Glasser/Johnson/Gossen management models—the five finger model of classroom management (see Figure 3.2).

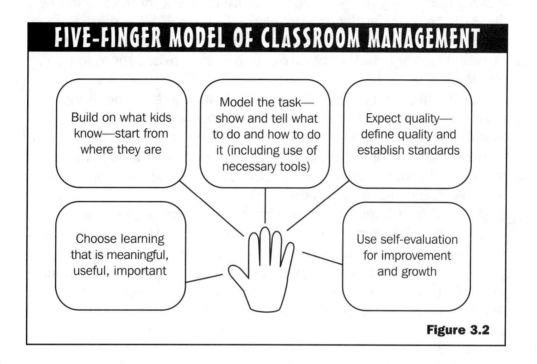

FIVE-FINGER MODEL OF CLASSROOM MANAGEMENT

Build on what kids know—start from where they are

Model the task—show and tell what to do and how to do it (including use of necessary tools)

Expect quality—define quality and establish standards

Choose learning that is meaningful, useful, important

Use self-evaluation for improvement and growth

Figure 3.2

The Thumb:
Making Learning Meaningful and Useful

I believe that my students produced work of higher quality once they understood the meaning, usefulness, or importance of the work we were doing or the concepts we were studying. I used a few different ways to help them see that they were being asked to do useful work. My favorite technique was to ask them. Here's an example.

At the beginning of the first unit of the year, I asked, "Why is it important to know how to evaluate the quality of the water that comes out of the faucet in your kitchen sink? What do you need to know about that water? How do you get that information? What scientific data do you need? What impact does water purity have on the quality of your life?"

A few units later I asked, "What products do you use every day that you might have to do without if we ran out of crude oil? Which of these products do you want to keep? Do you know how these products are made? Would you know how to use crude oil to make a new soft drink flavor or a new synthetic fabric?"

Friends of mine who teach English ask their students questions like, "What do you know about relationships between family members? What actions and thoughts help make families healthier? What actions hurt family relationships?" before they ask them to read plays like *King Lear* or *Hamlet* or a novel like *To Kill a Mockingbird*. Sometimes kids do not see the meaning or usefulness of their schoolwork or subject matter content because no one ever asked them to think about it.

Answering such questions helps students make connections between school and society and see the meaning of their classroom work. Choice theory teaches that we choose to do work that will add value to our lives or has meaning in our lives. Asking kids to make such connections helps them personalize the value or meaning of their work and *choose* to do the work.

Occasionally I felt that my students needed more information before they could appreciate the value of a topic. At such times I just came right out and told them what the relevance of the topic was. I might say, "I've seen what happens to a community when the nonrenewable resource it relies on as a major source of employment runs out. I've traveled through ghost towns in Illinois where lead was mined. The towns died when the lead ore was depleted. I've seen towns in Michigan fight to find new industries when their mines closed because the copper ran out. The chemistry we're about to study shows how these nonrenewable metals—lead and copper, among others—can be recycled and how recycling can create new industries—industries that some of you will very possibly be involved in. At the end of this unit I'll ask you to write a journal entry about how you think you could help a ghost town come back to life."

By sharing my knowledge base about the real-life value or implications of the subject matter, I help some of the kids choose to do the learning.

Sometimes I would introduce a topic with a statement like this one: "Let's face it. I want you to learn how to read bar graphs because I know you need this skill for the state achievement test (or the ACT test) and I want you to do well on that test. Doing well will improve your opportunities for future training or education. I want to help you have the widest range of opportunities available in the future." This last example may sound like teaching to the test. I see nothing wrong with that if it adds value to the lives of kids.

1. Assign an individual journal entry. Ask students to remember a really good school class/course that they have been involved in. Ask them, "What were your reasons for really liking this class? Why did you enjoy it so much? Why do you remember it so well? What did you do or what happened in this class that you really wish would happen more often in classes in school? Please have this writing done when you get to class tomorrow."

2. At the beginning of class the next day, ask each student to choose a partner and ask partners to share journal entries with each other and develop a list of general features of memorable and enjoyable classes.

3. Next, ask two pairs to get together, and then ask the foursomes to compare lists and develop one common list. One person in this foursome is the group conductor, who keeps the group on task and on time. A second group member is the journalist, who makes the official group copy of the list and reports the results to the class. The third member of the group is the dialogue director, who asks for input from all group members and checks for agreement and understanding. The fourth group member is the coach, who reminds group members to listen with understanding and use only encouraging words.

4. After the foursomes have had time to develop their lists, ask the journalists to report the results to the whole class. Record ideas on a sheet of chart paper. After all of the groups have reported, discuss the list with the class. One idea that may be common to all lists is that memorable classes are fun. With further probing, many students will say that these classes were fun because they gave the students skills or information that they could transfer to other settings or offered learning that the students really wanted.

5. Ask students to write a new, individual journal entry answering the questions, "Do classes that I really enjoy give me learning that I think is important and useful? How can I better understand the meaningfulness or importance of the learning that I am asked to do in all of my classes? What help do I need and who can help me? How can I ask for that help in an encouraging way? ◆

The Index Finger:
Building on Prior Knowledge

I wanted to help kids connect new learning with prior knowledge. I never assumed that I knew what they knew just because I was familiar with their prior curriculum. I asked the kids to tell me what they knew. Sometimes I used a KWL at the beginning of a content topic to accomplish this (see Figure 3.3).

KWL CHART

K What we think we know about this topic	W What we want to know about this topic	L What we have learned about this topic

Figure 3.3

We filled in the Ks and Ws before we began work on the content of the unit. The kids brainstormed Ks and Ws in small groups; then we shared and recorded answers to develop a class KWL chart. Sometimes the Ks revealed sound prior knowledge and understanding and provided an opportunity for advanced work. At other times the Ks indicated misconceptions and information gaps, in which case we remediated before moving on.

I never criticized or corrected answers while we brainstormed. I let further study help the students determine incomplete or incorrect prior learning. Following a formal study of a topic, we brainstormed Ls in small groups. As we discussed the Ls, the students (or I) would point out incorrect prior learning, if any. We recorded the correct information on the class KWL chart and crossed out inaccurate Ks.

The focus on Ls at the end of a unit reinforced our connection with prior studies. For example, I would say, "This is what we said we knew before we began working on this unit. Let's see where we are now." Looking back at the Ks as we recorded the Ls helped students see that improvement—correcting prior misunderstandings and building on prior knowledge—is an important component of learning. Seeking to improve adds quality to learning.

Another technique I used to gather information about prior knowledge was to have the students do a people search that focused on the upcoming topic. A people search can help kids focus on content, predict the priorities of a unit, and see examples of connections between the unit content and real life. Figure 3.4 shows a sample people search.

SAMPLE PEOPLE SEARCH

People Search: Quality Classrooms

Get a signature for each of the following items. A classmate may sign for only one item, so you'll need signatures from nine different classmates.

Find someone who . . .

can describe how she or he values a bit of learning from school	can "act out" the listening behavior of a quality teacher	knows how to get help when the going gets tough
can predict how he or she will use one specific learning from this class	can explain what a piece of quality writing looks like	is willing to describe an unexpected personal quality
can define three standards for quality work	can create a symbol that could be used to label quality work	can sing a few bars of "School Days"

Figure 3.4

1. Begin by giving each student a copy of the people search (see Fig. 3.3). Tell them, "Your job is to move around the room and find classmates who can explain, tell, draw, or sing what the people search asks for. One good way to get information is to offer to give it. Approach a classmate, use effective communication skills like smiling and using the person's name, and offer to give an answer and a signature. When someone does this for you, offer to reciprocate. Be sure that the person gives you the information with the signature."

2. Set a time limit for completion of the people search and ask students to start getting signatures. When everyone has successfully completed the job, ask students to give you their answers. Call on randomly selected students and ask each person, "Who signed your people search for (*choose an item*)?" The signer is then asked to explain, draw, act out, or sing the information in the answer. (Tell students before they begin the people search that they may be asked to contribute their answers or performances. Suggest that they not sign performance squares if they are unwilling to perform for the whole class.) Ask for voluntary additional information or ideas about each item. Spend forty minutes to one hour doing this activity.

3. By the time the answers and ideas for people search items are recorded, you can have a very good picture of the prior knowledge that the students have acquired about the topic the people search relates to, and the students have an opportunity to connect with and review that knowledge. ◆

Whichever technique I chose to use to find out what students already knew in order to build new learning on old, my key to success was in not assuming I knew what information the kids already had about a topic. I asked them for that information. Their answers gave me the most accurate possible picture about their prior learning. The process empowered them. In addition, by asking them what they knew, I gave them the signal that I respected them as learners and valued what they had to tell me.

The Middle Finger: Modeling the Task

The Process

Every classroom job involves two key factors: the process of doing the job and the tools needed to do it. Whenever I asked students to do a job, I did my best to describe and/or model it with them. We sometimes used T-charts to define and describe jobs. For example, we might use informal cooperative strategies to answer a question like, "What does checking for understanding look like and sound like? Do you just want to ask a teammate, 'Do you understand?' What might be a better way to do that?" We would script sample questions like, "Can you explain that in your own words? Can you paraphrase what Mary just said? Can you tell us how you solved that problem? Please describe your thinking process."

We would define and model body language—leaning in (or out), smiling, nodding, looking puzzled, giving "personal space" during thinking time, using encouraging gestures. We recorded our ideas on chart paper so we could post them in the room the next time we did a similar activity. Sometimes I asked students to role play new situations with me. We practiced for a few minutes while other students did individual work. Then we did the role play.

I modeled self-evaluation for students by sharing personal self-evaluations with them. I showed students samples of the kinds of products that I wanted from assigned activities. I suggested ways they could divide the work for a graphic. I might suggest that they ask a member of the group to be the artist, who sketched pictures in pencil. Another member of the group would be the calligrapher, who did the lettering, and the other group members would be the colorizers, who colored the work done by the artist.

I always asked students if they had enough information before they began a job. For example, "Did I explain that well enough? Is there anything you want me to go over again? Who can paraphrase what I said? What are you going to do first? How will you continue?" As we repeated types of activities, the modeling and direct instructing took less and less time. However, students never did a job without some prior instruction, modeling, and discussion. I never asked them to begin a job until they and I felt comfortable with their preparation. Students who feel confident that they know how to do a job will produce better quality work.

The Tools

Whenever students started a job, I also told them what tools were needed and where to find those tools. One of those tools was content knowledge. I told (or asked) them what content knowledge was needed to get the job done and where to find that information. I encouraged students to use the reference materials located on a shelf in my classroom. Some teachers have CD-ROM software that students can refer to. Students can also use textbooks and journals or course logs as reference sources. Other tools might include large sheets of newsprint and markers, model sets or other manipulatives, tape recorders, a camcorder with a monitor/VCR—the list could go on and on.

I always provided students with instructions about using special tools and demonstrated those tools for them. I often printed and laminated instructions for using equipment, which I would put on the wall beside the equipment or mount on the equipment for students to refer to if they forgot the oral directions. I asked students who knew how to use the equipment if they would be willing to help classmates who did not. Sometimes the kids even helped me—they knew more about some kinds of computer equipment than I did!

Job preparation was complete when students knew what to do, how to do it, what equipment or tools they needed, and how to use that equipment or those tools.

The Ring Finger:
Expecting and Establishing Quality Standards

From the first assignment of the year until the last day of school, I let students know that I expected high quality work. I applied Deming's philosophy of expecting the best that students were capable of producing and announcing my expectations. I did not simply say to students, "Go do quality work." First we defined quality. "What does quality mean?" I asked. Someone usually suggested we look it up in the dictionary, so I would ask a student sitting near the dictionary to do that. We found synonyms like "superiority" and "excellence." I asked students, "What does that really mean? What does superiority or excellence look like?" We brainstormed answers to those questions.

As often as possible we tied the definition of quality to the real world. For example, before I asked students to work in small groups to pick an element, research its properties, decide on an appropriate "monster movie" title based on those properties, and design a poster to publicize the movie, we looked at examples of real-world movie posters that the kids or I got from local theaters. We analyzed the features of those posters to decide why those movies were commercially successful. Or, before I asked students to work in small groups to write a nursery rhyme about the properties of a state of matter, we dissected some real nursery rhymes to decide why they had survived over the generations.

Rubrics

We used rubrics (written by others or developed by us) as evaluation tools for many kinds of work. My students learned to do quality writing by developing a rubric that described quality writing, by doing a writing assignment, by self-evaluating their writing using the rubric, and then by improving their writing sample.

Our high school English Department helped us develop the criteria for the writing rubric. Students asked if they could revise and simplify the English department rubric. They developed a rubric as their self-evaluation tool and for my use when I evaluated their writing (see Figure 3.5).

The students suggested the zero column in the rubric. They asked, "How will you let us know if you think our writing doesn't have *any* organization or focus or support? Don't we need a zero? Otherwise, if we see a one, we will think the focus or organization or support are there and just need to be improved."

I suggested we put the "three" column on the left—next to the criteria. I explained that putting the zero column to the left of the three columns might have us focus on the negative when we wanted our focus to be on the positive (we read from left to right and I wanted the kids to read the positives first). The kids agreed that my argument made sense.

We used this rubric to evaluate all writing assignments. Student writing showed continued improvement because students knew the standards for quality writing and used those standards to self-evaluate and improve.

SAMPLE WRITING RUBRIC

Where Does My Writing Fit?

	0	1	2	3
Focus clear point of view	missing	confused, shifting, or disjointed	sometimes cloudy; reader may need to assume position	clear and specifically stated throughout
Support elaboration or exploration of major points	missing	inaccurate or missing more than 50 percent of the time	at least 50 percent of major points "backed up"	each major point "backed up" with two to three pieces of accurate evidence
Organization logical flow of ideas; clear plan	missing	connections are missing or unclear	at least 50 percent of points connected; transitions may be weak	all points connected and signaled with transitions or clear indicators
Conventions use of standard English	jabberwocky	major errors that confuse meaning; ineffective sentence structure	some minor errors; no more than one or two major errors	few minor errors, if any; clear, precise vocabulary and sentence structure

Figure 3.5

Activity 7

1. Ask students to create a rubric for something that is familiar to them and that they think is fun. You may decide to do a brainstorm with them before they start working on the rubric to develop a list of suggested topics. Suggest that they may want to do a rubric for a pizza, a specific kind of party, a picnic—any fun topic will do.

2. Students will write the rubrics in groups of three. One member of the group will be the assessment coordinator, who will keep the group focused, on task, and on time. A second group member will be the publisher, who will record the official group copy of the rubric and report on the results to the rest of the class. The final member of the group will be the manager, who will keep members focused on listening to each other and using encouraging words.

3. Groups will begin by choosing the rubric topic. Members of the group will then brainstorm the criteria for the topic. For a pizza, for example, members of the group might decide that the criteria are the crust, sauce, cheese, other toppings, and taste. The criteria are the key features of the thing or event being evaluated. The assessment coordinator will begin the brainstorm by saying, "I think that one criterion for _(a pizza)_ is _(the crust)_. The publisher will answer, "I like that idea because _(the crust holds the whole pizza together)_." The manager will write down the criterion and the reasoning.

Criterion	Reasoning

4. The roles will then rotate one place to the right around the group. The rotation will continue until each member of the group has had a chance to contribute two criteria to the list. Then members of the group will contribute ideas for criteria at random until no one has a new criterion.

5. The group will look over the list of ideas and decide which criteria to use in the rubric. They will begin to build the rubric by asking the publisher to list the criteria on a sheet of paper.

Each member of the group will then develop individual indicators for each criterion. Each student will have a pad of small Post-it notes and will write each indicator on its own Post-it. Students may do this part of the activity outside of class.

6. When the individual work on indicators is finished, group members will compare ideas and decide on consensus indicators. The publisher will record these consensus indicators on the group rubric. The finished product will look like the rubric in figure 3.4.

7. Each group will present its rubric to the whole class. Groups will self-evaluate by answering these questions: What did we learn about making rubrics? What part of the process that we used do we want to keep? What do we want to do differently next time? What did we do well as a team? How can we improve our teamwork? ◆

Journals

Another way I helped kids define quality was to give them a quote from Myron Tribus, a follower of Dr. Deming. Tribus said, "Quality is what makes it possible for your customer to have a love affair with your product or service." I asked each student to write an individual journal entry answering the following questions: What features of your classroom work or performance will help me, the customer for that work or performance, have a love affair with it. If you were the customer for your own work or performance, would you have a love affair with it, or would the attraction be infatuation and quickly fade? How can you improve your work or performance to encourage this "love affair"? What is one improvement you are willing to try?

I then suggested that the students use this journal entry to decide on personal work or performance goals for class and develop a plan to reach their goals. Students *can* do quality work. I believe that the key to getting them to do it is to ask for it, to define it, to show them real-world examples of quality in the kinds products that they are making, to help them analyze the quality features of those real-world products, and to give them quality standards to work toward. I also believe that every product we make and every performance we do can be improved, and that students can be encouraged to self-evaluate and decide how they could improve "next time." Doing the best job they can "this time" and then deciding how that could be improved "next time" produces an outward spiral of quality work in the classroom.

The Little Finger:
Self-Evaluation for Improvement and Growth

I have referred to self-evaluation several times in this chapter. I believe that teaching students how to self-evaluate effectively is one of the most important pieces of teaching that can occur in the classroom. Students who have never been asked to self-evaluate may initially be uncomfortable with the concept. Although my high school students were quite accustomed to external evaluation, they resisted self-evaluating. External evaluations often tend to be critical and judgmental. Even "constructive criticism" may result in defensive behaviors that can interfere with growth. The kids and I worked hard to internalize the concept that we were not going to grow and improve by blaming others for our problems or by making excuses for not reaching personal goals. I posted the following sign on days when students were setting goals and planning for future growth:

The sign helped remind us that defensiveness could block real growth toward quality.

Because most of my students had little experience self-evaluating, I provided a variety of tools and suggestions to get them started. (Examples of these tools and suggestions can be found in Part III of *A Multiple Intelligences Road to a Quality Classroom.*)

Students may be given a fairly extensive list of effective school behaviors like being in class every day, being ready to start on time, asking for help when they need it, asking good questions, and persisting when learning gets tough. They may also be asked to rate themselves as usually using a behavior, occasionally using a behavior, or not using a behavior—yet. They may be asked to write a journal entry describing their best actions, thoughts, and cooperation during an activity, and identifying what they would like to improve when they do the next activity. They may be asked what letter grade they believe they are earning in the class and what qualities of their academic work, teamwork, and effective school behavior support that grade. Students are reminded that the heart of self-evaluation is asking, "What did I want? What was my goal? What did I do to get there? **DID WHAT I DID WORK?**" If the answer to the last question is "No," they should ask themselves, "What other behaviors might I use to reach my goal? Do I know what else I might try, do I need help learning new behaviors?"

I believe that self-evaluation is like any other skill—the more people practice it, the more skillful they become at it. I asked students to self-evaluate at the end of each activity. Sometimes they did the self-evaluation individually and sometimes in small groups. I used two basic sets of frequent, repetitive self-evaluative questions (see Figure 3.6).

Both sets of questions helped students focus on the goal for the activity, the behaviors they used as they worked toward that goal, the effectiveness of those behaviors, the quality of the products, personal

SAMPLE SELF-EVALUATIVE QUESTIONS

Set 1

What did you want to do and/or produce?

What did you want that performance and/or product to be?

What did you do well?

What was strong about your performance and/or product?

What would you do differently next time?

How would your changes improve your performance and/or product?

What help do you need and who do you see helping you?

Set 2

What did you want to do and/or produce?

Who did you want to be?

As you worked—what were your best actions?

What were your best thoughts?

In what ways were you capable (or free, or accepted, or playful)?

Were you the student you wanted to be?

How could you be that student next time?

What help do you need and who do you see helping you?

Figure 3.6

IRI/SkyLight Training and Publishing, Inc.

growth and improvement, and becoming the students they wanted to be. I read my own self-evaluation to students to model the process. I did this every time I asked them to self-evaluate during the first month of school and occasionally after that. This showed them that I valued self-evaluation, that I believed in it as a tool for personal growth, that I used self-evaluation and looked for ways to improve how I taught (even after thirty years), and that I was doing the same job that I was asking them to do.

I believe that self-evaluation can be used to, as Perry Good says, "bump up" students' levels of perceptions about themselves. I asked students very concrete self-evaluative questions like, "Is what you are doing producing quality?" I also asked them more abstract self-evaluative questions like, "Are you being the student you want to be in this class? Who is that student? Someone who is in control? Someone who is successful? Someone who does quality work?"

Self-evaluation becomes a more effective tool for choosing responsible classroom behaviors if it is used to focus on present positive behaviors and accomplishments before being used as a tool for change and improvement. Teachers who focus on self-evaluation as something that a student does when he or she has "misbehaved," and who use it only as a tool for "discipline," miss out on its effectiveness as a tool for producing quality. They are like cooks who use their microwave ovens only to heat leftovers. They get results, and those results may be acceptable, but the results are not products with which to have a love affair.

Both W. E. Deming and Dr. William Glasser stress the lack of coercion as a key component of quality management. A classroom that uses the five-finger model for quality will be a coercion-free classroom. A classroom leader will not even consider using coercion if students

- understand the value or usefulness of what they are asked to do;

- understand how this task or learning connects with prior knowledge;

- see the job modeled;

- see examples of the products they have been asked to make;

- know what tools or equipment they need and how to use them;

- know the standards for quality in the job they have been asked to do or the product they have been asked to make;

- reach quality by self-evaluating and improving; and

- feel physically, emotionally, and collegially safe.

Student behaviors that may influence a teacher to become coercive will rarely, if ever, occur in a five-finger classroom. Students engage themselves in the business of the classroom willingly, enthusiastically, and completely. The teacher feels the quality as she facilitates and mediates learning—quality in working relationships, quality in desire, and quality in production. Lead managing is steering down the center of the quality learning lane.

Tuning the Engine and Checking the Tires

Choice Theory in the Classroom

The best drivers I know take really good care of their cars. Before they start on a long trip, they make sure their engines are tuned and they check their tires to be sure they have just enough air. According to choice theory, the basic needs we all have—survival, belonging, power, freedom, and fun—are the sparkplugs that ignite our behaviors. Just as a sparkplug ignites the fuel in an engine, the desire to satisfy one or more of these basic needs impels us to act. Behaviors are made up of four parts—just as there are four tires on a car. We feel most in control of our lives when the tires are relatively balanced and are full of "good" air—behavior that gets us what we want without being unlawful, irresponsible, unreasonable, or unrealistic. Won't teaching and learning be more effective if we ensure that everything under the hood of the classroom car is in tune and if we check the tires before starting a learning journey?

USING CHOICE THEORY

Looks Like	Sounds Like
• few posted classroom rules	• "I chose to _(do something)_ because . . ."
• no "star" or "penalty" charts	• "Let's talk about it."
• "total behavior" poster (for example, a behavior car)	• "It's OK to disagree."
• students and teacher share the focus	• "We can work it out."
• students coaching each other	• "Is it responsible? reasonable? realistic? ethically/legally right?
• calm, purposeful activity	• engaged, happy, work-focused buzz

Figure 4.1

Principles of Choice Theory

Basic Needs

I believe that productive, growth-enhancing choice of effective behaviors and self-evaluation of whether or not those behaviors are working is best done by people who have some knowledge of choice theory (as explained by Dr. William Glasser) and who have learned how to use it to take more effective control of their lives. Choice theory, or control theory, to use its other name, is rooted in the idea that all human behavior is driven by five basic needs—survival, power, belonging, freedom, and fun.

Survival. The "old brain" need, survival, is strongly biological. We are unaware of some of the ways that our bodies help us meet this need—regulating body temperature, digesting food, adjusting breathing and heart rate, producing more or less adrenaline. We are very aware of other physical signals—feeling thirsty or sleepy or wakeful. We are aware of the need to reproduce—to ensure survival of the species. I think that we also act to satisfy our need to survive when we buy clothing that is climate appropriate, pay the rent or mortgage to provide ourselves with shelter, save money to give ourselves financial security, learn how to cook so that we can prepare the food that we need to survive, visit the dentist to maintain good oral health, have regular checkups with the family physician and take prescribed medications to maintain good physical health, and do some kind of physical exercise to promote general fitness.

I believe that school kids choose some of their behaviors to promote academic survival. Students who believe that post–high school education is the key to "being what they want to be when they grow up" will do just about any job teachers ask them to do or learn just about anything that teachers ask them to learn. They want more than to just pass; they want to receive high marks. I used to ask myself how some of my teachers "made me" perform the work that they asked me to do. My choice theory explanation is that I was internally motivated to do the required work in their classes because I wanted to survive academically and because I wanted to feel competent (power need).

Power. Choice theory explains that the other four needs are "new brain," or psychological, needs. The need for power, a need that I believe I helped satisfy when I survived academically, is the need to feel competent, capable, "in charge," in control, and recognized as someone who can contribute valuable products or ideas.

As I write these words I am satisfying my need for power in several ways. I feel competent and capable in writing. I believe that I have the vocabulary and writing skills to communicate my thoughts so that others will understand them. I am in charge of this project—no one else is telling me what to write or when to write it. I believe that the ideas I am communicating will help other teachers experience more success and happiness in their classrooms, so I believe that the ideas are valuable. I feel self-powerful.

I also feel capable of using my computer and my word-processing software to do the writing. I believe that I know the machine and the software well enough to be able to use them efficiently. I feel object-powerful.

I model the ideas in this book whenever I teach. I find that using the quality classroom approach results in a high degree of participant involvement. Students choose to do what I ask them to do because they believe that I am asking them to do useful learning. Because they are so committed, involved, and cooperative, I feel other-people powerful.

Students feel powerful when they know that others will listen to their ideas and opinions. (Really listening to another person is one of the most empowering behaviors.) In cooperative learning activities, each student is expected to contribute ideas, opinions, and learnings to the group, to listen to the other students in the group, and to paraphrase or expand on the ideas of other group members. The teacher listens to ideas that groups and individuals contribute to the whole class' understanding of topics. Being listened to gives students and the teacher a feeling of competence, recognition, and importance. Students who are provided with the opportunity to work in a cooperative setting usually thrive in school, and I believe that their achievement is, in part, based in the satisfaction of their need for power.

Belonging. Another psychological need is the need for love and belonging. We know we are satisfying this need when we feel accepted, welcomed, and included. I feel most loved and accepted when I'm with my husband, family, or close friends. I also satisfy this need when participants in the courses I teach ask me out to lunch or dinner, invite me to join their conversations during breaks, or come to class early or stay late to talk about personal concerns or interests. I help students meet this need by greeting them at the door, saying good-bye to them as they leave, celebrating success with them, and recognizing them when I meet them outside of class. Students tell me that cooperative learning groups and activities also help them feel that they belong in the classroom—that they are members of a learning team, not just individuals who are going it alone. David and Roger Johnson, among others, report that students who feel isolated and alone are most at risk for failing in school. On the other hand, students who can satisfy their need for belonging in school are very likely to succeed.

Freedom. The psychological need for freedom is satisfied by making choices. I made lots of choices before writing this book. I decided what to include, where to work, when to work, and how long to work each day. I wanted to be free *to* concentrate, free *to* write at my own pace, free *from* distractions, free *from* other responsibilities.

Kids can be given choices even in very structured classrooms. I wanted kids to demonstrate their learning in a variety of ways. If I wanted a graphic organizer, I would ask them to give me information as words and pictures, I would suggest a few graphic organizers that they could use, and I would let them make the final choice. For comparing and contrasting, I might suggest a Venn diagram, a fishbone, or a T-chart. If I wanted a rhythmic product, I might suggest a "rap" song, a poem, or a mnemonic. If I wanted them to "act out" information, I might suggest a puppet show, a pantomime, or a captioned "silent movie." For long-term cooperative tasks, I assigned students to groups, told them what roles they needed to have group members fill, and then let them pick who would fill which role. For short-term activities, I often let them pick their own partners. When I assigned work that involved mathematical solutions, I told kids, "There is no one right way to get the answers. Just be sure to show me your method. Any method of doing the work that gives you a correct answer is fine." Kids felt free *to* make some choices and free *from* being regimented and bossed. The belief that the freedom need was being met helped them choose effective, in-control class-room behaviors.

Fun. Finally, we all need to experience fun. Fun can be a reward for learning. Fun is also a product of play. Fun, to me, is strongly associated with delight and enchantment. Kids in classes I have taught often said they thought doing lab was fun. They loved watching what happened when they mixed things together. Some of them would act out "mad scientist" behavior that they had seen in movies. The gasps of delight and cries of joy that I heard when we mixed substances that glowed in the dark told me that the kids had fun doing that activity.

Kids—and adults—also have fun working together. They enjoy the social interchanges. They sometimes get silly—making faces, creating puns, telling jokes. I loved watching kids produce graphics—they have so much fun with the colored markers. Just because I asked kids to learn important, serious concepts did not mean that the learning process had to be joyless.

A teacher recently asked for help trouble shooting. She knew choice theory, and she lead-managed in her classroom. The trouble, as she perceived it, was that her students were not as engaged in learning as they could be. I asked her, "On a scale of zero to four, how much power do you think your kids feel in your classroom?" She said, "Oh, probably a three." We analyzed belonging and freedom, and the results were the same. Then we got to fun. I could almost see a light click on in her head. She said, "I think my kids are getting a zero or a one in fun in most of the activities we do. I think we need to have more fun."

1. Begin this activity with a frontload—a lecturette that outlines and basically describes the five basic needs as defined by Dr. William Glasser. Then read a children's story to the class and ask them to focus on (and maybe jot down a few notes about) the ways in which the characters meet their needs for survival, power, belonging, freedom, and fun. Choose a story in which the characters start out in conflict and finish in friendship. A story that I really like to use is *The Three Little Wolves* and the *Big Bad Pig* by Trivizas and Oxenbury.

2. After the students have heard the story, assign them to groups of three. One member of the group is the conductor, who keeps the group focused, on task, and on time. A second member of the group is the journalist, who records the official group copy of the assignment. The third member of the group is the diplomat, who encourages everyone to participate and helps everyone remember to listen attentively to everyone else and celebrate success.

3. Ask groups to list how the characters in the story met their five basic needs. Ask them to use a grid or fishbone graphic organizer to make the list. Before groups begin their work, ask for volunteers or randomly selected students to review the five basic needs. Give groups about ten to fifteen minutes to make their lists.

4. Do a wraparound to collect ideas about how the characters in the story met their needs. Record the answers in a grid or fishbone on chart paper or on the blackboard. Then ask groups to self-evaluate by answering these questions: How did doing this activity help you understand the basic needs? As you worked together, how did you meet your need for belonging? What did you do to feel capable (powerful)? What choices did you make—how did you meet your need for freedom? What was fun? Did the group get silly? Is this classroom a place where you can meet your needs?

5. Ask groups to celebrate success. ◆

Everyone has an individual, unique needs profile. We have individual, personal drives to satisfy our needs—some of us need more power than others, some need less fun, and so on. Students vary in their needs for power, belonging, freedom, and fun. I wanted to help all students satisfy their strongest need at least part of the time in the classroom. I thought that would help all students choose more effective, responsible behaviors. I analyzed lesson structures for probable need satisfaction. I ask students to include a description of need satisfaction as part of their evaluation of lessons. I asked them, "As you did this activity, when did you feel capable and in charge? When did you feel accepted and involved in the class or in your group? When did you make choices, feel free to decide what to do or how to do it, or feel free from being bossed? When did you feel silly, feel really engaged in the task, or feel an energy surge as you learned?" I recorded their answers and used the information to revise future lessons. I did this need satisfaction analysis because I wanted to help students choose behaviors that would help them be in effective control of their learning.

Behavior

So how do we satisfy our basic needs? How do we feel included, liked, powerful, free, and playful, joyful, or delightful? Choice theory says that we meet our needs by behaving. All behavior is made up of four key components: acting (or doing), thinking, feeling (emotions), and physiology (body talk or healthing). All four components are present in every behavior. When choice theorists say, "Behave," they do not mean, "Mind your mother." They are saying, "Do, act, feel, and health." When they ask, "How did you behave?," they are asking for a description of the doing, feeling, thinking, and healthing package. The four components are not necessarily balanced in a given behavior. Most behaviors are stronger in some aspects and weaker in others. Choice theory asks us to remember that all four are present in every behavior, and that we will be in more effective control of our lives when we understand this.

Choice theory uses a car metaphor to explain the interconnectedness of the four components of behavior. It says that total behavior is like a front-wheel-drive car. The front wheels of the car are acting and thinking. The back wheels are feeling and healthing. Here's a sketch showing the wheel arrangement.

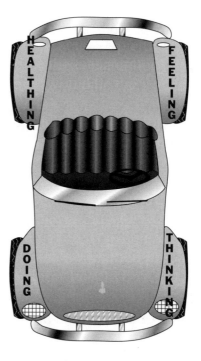

Feeling and Healthing. According to choice theory, a person is always aware of how she feels. If her feelings are painful, she can change what she is feeling by changing how she is acting or what she is thinking. She may be aware of how she is healthing—but she will usually not pay a lot of attention to body talk unless it is negative. Knowing what is happening with feeling and healthing—acknowledging and accurately identifying feelings and body talk—helps a person choose more effective behaviors. As long as feelings and health are positive, a person will continue using her old, organized behaviors.

Negative feelings, such as displeasure, anger, or frustration, or negative body signals, such as headaches or stomach cramps, can initiate a search for new behaviors. Negative body signals may result from a person's unwillingness to acknowledge negative emotions.

Choice theory also maintains that we always want to work our way out of pain and into pleasure. If we feel powerless to change an ongoing, unpleasant situation in life, a situation in which we feel frustrated or stressed or unhappy, we may try to ignore the negative emotional signals we feel. When we do this, our behavior system may create a negative healthing behavior to get us out of the situation and back in control of our lives.

Kids who are unsuccessful in school may not admit that they feel incompetent or incapable as learners. They may not admit, even to themselves, that they do not have much fun in school. They may, however, be absent fairly often because of severe headaches, vague flulike symptoms, or even ulcers. Their systems are supplying them with body-talk behaviors that will keep them home, where they feel more capable, more loved, and where they have more fun. If these kids can find ways to meet their needs in school, if school becomes a place where they feel more capable, accepted, and where they enjoy themselves more, these sicking behaviors may disappear. School as a need-fulfilling place will become a place where they want to be—a strong picture in their quality worlds.

Thinking and Doing. I used the front-wheel-drive car to analyze the effectiveness of my classroom behaviors, and to decide when to continue using a behavior and when to try a different behavior or learn a new one. At the end of a class period I would ask myself, "How do I feel right now, and what is my body telling me?" This *thinking* component of behavior started the analysis. Sometimes I answered, "I feel satisfied with the results of the lesson; I'm happy. I'm very excited about the work the kids produced. I just feel all snuggly and content about it and my body feels relaxed and comfortable."

My next question would be, "So do I know what we did, what our *actions* were today, so I can do the same thing to learn new information or to repeat this lesson?"

At other times, I answered, "I'm feeling edgy and discontented. I am not happy right now. I feel a knot in my stomach, and a vague headache." At those times, I would ask myself, "*Think* about what happened. What is it that I don't like. Is the learning inaccurate or incomplete? Did students seem to be confused about what I wanted them to do? Did they stay on task, or did they choose behaviors that were not productive? What do I want to *do* to find out the reasons for the lesson not being particularly successful?"

I knew that in order to change what I was doing to facilitate learning I usually needed to think about possible strategies, analyze their possibilities for being effective, and choose a behavior to use. My feeling and healthing would follow along. I would feel better, emotionally and physically, by thinking about more effective ways to act and then carrying out those actions.

1. When students in a class seem distracted, absent-minded, or fidgety, their bodies may be telling them that some physical activity would feel good. When you observe this behavior in the classroom, say, "Everybody—stand up. Stretch your hands above your heads—stretch as far as you can. Now kick your left foot up and catch it with your right hand. Do that five times. Switch—kick your right foot up and catch it with your left hand. Do that five times. Put your hands on your waist and bend to the right five times—front five times—left five times. (Actually count out "one-two-three-four-five" for the repetitions.) Make eye contact with a friend across the room and high five with your right hand—now with your left hand. Now sit down."

2. Say, "We just used a behavior that focused our attention on our acting wheel. Please do a journal entry that answers these questions: As you were doing the actions, what were you thinking? What were your emotions—what were you feeling? What was your body saying—what were you healthing?

3. Ask students to share answers with a neighbor. ◆

I was more effective in the classroom, had more positive emotions, and was physically healthier when I learned to "drive my own car." Once I really bought into the idea that changing what I was doing and thinking could change my feelings, I became much less focused on "feeling sad, angry, frustrated, or down" when I had those feelings. I became pretty good at answering the following questions: What did I do and what was the thinking behind the doing that led to those painful feelings? What do I do and how do I think when I'm feeling good? Which of those actions and thoughts might help me now? I did not hide from negative feelings—I just chose to use behaviors that would help change those feelings.

Putting Choice Theory to Work in the Classroom

Our painful feelings or poor health frequently result from a failure to control someone else—to make him or her do what we want. Choice theory teaches that the only person I can control is myself. As I take in information from the world around me, I constantly filter it through personal knowledge and values. I compare what I'm getting from the world with pictures I have stored in my brain—pictures about what I want or who I want to be. If my perception is that I'm getting what I want and being the person I want to be, I'm happy. I will choose to keep doing what I have been doing to be happy and content.

According to choice theory, the pictures we have of what we want from the world and who we want to be make up our "quality worlds." Because each person is a unique individual with a unique way of perceiving the world and a unique set of knowledge and value filters, we each have a unique quality world. We each choose behaviors we think will help us get what we want to have or be who we want to be.

I wanted to be a capable, including, happy teacher. If I saw my students producing work that demonstrated useful learning, saw them using effective teamwork skills, heard invitations to see their work or join their groups for short periods of time, I felt capable, including and included, and happy. I got what I wanted, and I was happy with the behaviors that I was using. If I saw students producing work that demonstrated confused learning, bickering, wandering around instead of forming cohesive groups, or doing lots of "off task" things, I was not happy. I felt that I had not structured a real learning activity. I used these occasions to learn an effective new behavior.

Instead of just assuming that "the kids were being disrespectful and lazy" or "I couldn't trust kids to do as they were told," instead of delivering a lecture on responsible behavior, I asked the kids what was happening. I told myself that I could control my behavior—not theirs. I would behave to get what I really wanted—my quality world pictures—and they would behave to get theirs. I knew that we all saw what was happening in the classroom differently, and I did not want to assume that I could accurately guess what the kids were seeing. So I said something like, "I had a picture of what would be happening in the classroom when we did this lesson. That's not what I'm seeing right now. I want to see some learning happening. Do I need to go back and explain what to do and how to do it? Did I not give you a good enough model of how to do this lesson? What can we do to get some learning to happen?"

When kids were off task or uncooperative it was usually because they did not really understand the job. Sometimes kids just wanted to spend time venting about things that had happened outside the classroom. Sometimes they wanted time to do "what they wanted to do." We found ways to restructure learning activities so that the learning got done, cooperation was enhanced, and they got a few moments to just kick back, relax, and recharge their mental batteries. I helped them stay focused on learning, and they were willing to maintain the focus because they had success in the class as a picture in their quality worlds.

Activity 10

1. Revisit the story that you read to the class to help them learn the five basic needs. Ask students if they want to hear the story again or if they want to summarize the story. Do the reading or summarizing. Then ask, "When the characters were in conflict at the beginning of the story, what were they doing to try to control each other? Were they trying to use coercion? Did that work? Did they help each other meet their needs? What about at the end of the story? Were the characters trying to control each other, or was each character focusing on effective control of his or her own behavior? What were they doing to help each other meet their needs? Had they moved into each other's quality worlds?"

2. Ask students to work in the groups of three that picked the need-satisfying behaviors out of the story the first time you used it. Give groups time to discuss the answers and then ask each one to report its answers to the rest of the class. Point out that painful behaviors like angering, avoiding, withdrawing, and

excluding are less effective than pleasant behaviors like encouraging, including, joining, and engaging. Focus on the feeling wheel during the painful and pleasant behaviors.

3. Ask each student to write an individual journal entry containing a plan to help her remember that she can only control herself and that acting on what she can control contributes to feeling capable while acting on what she cannot control contributes to feelings of inadequacy and anger. Ask students to invent personal trigger words for "can control" and "can't control." Suggest that they practice using those trigger words to help them gain more effective control of their own total behaviors. ◆

Understanding choice theory can help us all lead happier, healthier, more successful lives. Classrooms can be more successful when both the students and the teacher know some choice theory. Remembering these basics can help a teacher manage a quality classroom. All of our behaviors are purposeful, internally motivated, and the best that we know at the time. We always choose to do our best—we set out to be good, effective people. We are capable of learning new behaviors, and we will tolerate the discomfort that comes with learning new behaviors if we see that they will give us something we want. We choose our behaviors to satisfy our needs for survival, belonging, power, freedom, and fun. Our behaviors consist of four components—doing, thinking, feeling, and healthing. We always know how we feel. We cannot change our feelings by choosing new feelings; we can change our feelings by changing what we do and think. We need to recognize and deal with our painful feelings, or our behavior systems will find a way to force that recognition. We can control only what we do—not what anyone else does.

If we are a picture in someone's quality world, we may be able to influence her behavior. We can be more happy, successful, and effective if we recognize what we can control and what we cannot control, do our best to control what we can and be who we want to be, and stop worrying about what we cannot control. If we keep the engine tuned in our behavior cars, if we choose responsible behaviors to effectively meet our own needs, and if we remember to balance the tires—doing, acting, feeling, and healthing—our behaviors will help us get what we want without hurting anyone else. That is the essence of responsible behavior, in and out of the classroom.

The philosophy underlying choice theory is that people are basically good; we want to do the right thing. When we use a behavior to satisfy one or more needs, we choose the best behavior we have to get the job done. We never choose to do the worst that we can do.

We can always learn new behaviors to satisfy our needs—and we will be willing to learn those new behaviors if the old ones don't give us the results we want.

As a very young teacher, I wanted to help the kids in my classes learn the content they were expected to learn. I knew that I needed to keep some "order" in the classroom to do that. I still believed, however, that a very effective way to help kids learn was to deliver very well orchestrated, logical (to me), focused, and long lectures to large groups of students while they took notes that were complete, clear, accurate, and useful. That was how I had learned, and I did not know about learning styles (and multiple intelligences theory had not yet come into being), so I believed that all students would learn what I wanted them to learn if I could just lecture clearly enough. Some students were very quiet and looked very attentive. Others got restless, fidgeted in their desks, fell asleep, or started whispering to their classmates and passing notes.

To maintain "good learning conditions," I preached the value of self-control and courtesy to these disorderly kids. They usually acted in ways that I found more acceptable for a short time. The inattentive behaviors tended to reappear as time passed. As I learned more about learning styles and multiple intelligences, I realized that I needed to use different strategies to help kids learn. I learned more about structuring cooperative lessons, helping kids use graphic organizers, including musical and/or rhythmic ways of learning, doing kinesthetic activities (including use of manipulatives), and including logging or journaling activities to enhance student learning. I learned that interested, involved adults found their attention wandering from even a brilliant lecture after about twenty minutes, and that kids have even shorter attention spans than adults—in other words, short lectures work and long ones do not.

As I learned new classroom strategies and made them part of my teaching repertoire, I found that kids did become more engaged learners, learned better, remembered their learnings longer, were happier in the classroom, and that "discipline problems" disappeared. In choice theory terms, at the beginning of my teaching career I used the best behaviors I knew for helping kids learn. I used behaviors that I had learned by watching my teachers and seeing what worked for them—or at least what worked for me in their classrooms. I knew that the strategies I used were not working for all kids. I did not change what I was doing because I was not aware of any behaviors that were better than the ones I was already using.

When I discovered new information about learning styles, I chose to learn new behaviors that were more congruent with those theories. The new behaviors were more effective, so I changed what I was doing in the classroom.

Choice theory teaches that a person will learn new behaviors and will be willing to change when she or he believes that the change will have a payoff. "What's in it for me?" is a question that I asked myself, sometimes unconsciously, as I tried new behaviors in my classroom. The changed student behavior gave me the answer—because kids were happier in the classroom and were no longer "disruptive," I was having more fun. Because I perceived that kids were doing what I asked them to do and were learning more, I believed that I was a more effective facilitator and mediator of learning, and I felt more capable—more powerful. Kids were making more choices in the classroom. They were choosing short-term learning partners or roles within long-term cooperative teams. They were choosing which graphic organizer to use to make their learning visible. They had some freedom to get out of their chairs and move around the room—to stand at the lab tables or sit on the floor to work.

And I had more freedom because they had more freedom. I had the freedom to move around the room, facilitate effective teamwork, mediate accurate learning, and spend time writing in my journal. Kids greeted me when they came into the room, said goodbye when they left, came early and left late, wanted to be in the room for some extra learning before and after school, and wanted me to be a part of their group. The feeling of "we're all in this together" was one of inclusion, of being a part of a family of learners. So the changes that I made resulted in enhancement of the classroom as a *need-satisfying* place for me. The answer to "What's in it for me?" was that I was meeting my needs more effectively. That helped me sustain my desire for change and my willingness to practice new behaviors.

I taught my kids about choice theory, so they knew about the behavior car, the basic needs, and quality world pictures. I asked them, "Are your behaviors in this class different from the ones that you use in other classes? Tell me specifically—what do you do that is different and what do you think that is different?"

Kids said things like, "I think I can learn in this class." "I come to this class; that's different for me." "I get to work in groups in this class." "I get to sing/draw/move around in this class." "I get to make some choices in this class."

I asked, "What about doing your work? Do you study and come prepared?" Most of them said that they did. I asked, "Do you study and come prepared for all of your classes?" Some said that they did; others said that this was the only class for which they did much, if any, work. I asked, "What's different about this class? What are your reasons for choosing to do your work for this class?" They told me that they knew it would help them be more successful—that they knew they could do at least competent work in the class and they also believed that, with time and effort, they could do quality work.

Most kids will become quality students when they work in quality classrooms. They will learn new behaviors that will help them do quality learning because they will feel that they are capable, respected, included, and happy individuals who belong to a community of quality learners.

CHAPTER

5

Adjusting the Seats

Cooperative Learning

When I'm looking for a new car, I always take the time to sit in all the seats. I want everyone who will ride in the car to be comfortable—the passengers as well as the driver. I want everyone to have plenty of personal space, seats that are high and soft enough, and safety belts that fit without strangling or binding. My reasoning is that when a group of us is going somewhere in the car, we will be much happier travelers if all of us are comfortable. When I go for a test drive, I also listen to the noise of the car and the quality of the sound system. I ask myself if a group of travelers would be able to travel together comfortably. Before we start up our classroom cars, do we provide kids with a comfortable environment and helpful traveling companions? Cooperative learning groups can provide a setting that helps kids satisfy all of their needs and experience more successful learning.

COOPERATIVE LEARNING

Looks Like	Sounds Like
• kids working in pairs or small groups	• low hum or buzz of voices
• team flags or banners on the walls or ceilings	• teams doing "success" cheers
• small clusters of desks (no rows)	• "Let's all sign this."
• kids sitting face-to-face	• "Do we all agree?"
• kids pointing to a common book or paper	• "I heard you say . . . This is my thought."
• poster: We Sink or Swim Together	• "I know we can."

Figure 5.1

Throughout my career as a classroom teacher, I wanted to give kids opportunities to work together. Kids in my classes worked with lab partners when they did experiments, and the partners seemed to reinforce each other's strengths and help each other with personal weaknesses. I assigned lab partners. I tried to match up students who were high science achievers with those who did not achieve as well. I often noticed that the students who took longer to grasp mathematical concepts were better at manipulating laboratory equipment, and vice versa. (I didn't know at the time that I was getting information about the mathematical and kinesthetic intelligences.) These lab teams worked well because each person perceived that she was more successful with her partner than she would be on her own.

When kids were doing nonlab work, I did not apply what I knew about the success of these assigned partners. I described the task and then just told kids, "Pick one or two other students to work with and get the job done."

I was not very happy with the results. Students often picked their best buddies as teammates and spent lots of time off task. Some students wanted to work in groups of seven or eight. Other students were never picked to be members of a group. Although I thought that kids could learn better in groups, I did not know how to facilitate the process.

The Cooperative Learning Model

Then I discovered cooperative learning. The model in which I received my initial training was developed by Roger and David Johnson. The Johnson brothers are social scientists who focus on finding ways to reduce violence, improve conflict management, promote appreciation for cultural diversity and tolerance for cultural differences, and encourage kids to treat each other more respectfully. Their cooperative learning model tells teachers to

- assign students to small teams or groups;

- make the groups as heterogeneous as possible;

- assign roles within the groups so that students share leadership responsibilities;

- explicitly teach and model positive social skills so that kids learn how to work together;

- structure tasks so that students perceive that they can be more successful together than alone;

- monitor groups as they work together;

- facilitate group functioning as needed;

- mediate successful and accurate content learning; and

- provide time for groups to process—to reflect on their own learnings and functioning.

The Johnsons are not as concerned with *content* learning as they are with *process* learning. They believe that students need to be taught how to work together and how to cooperate, because, for all of our apparent focus on winners and losers, real progress in our society results from cooperative efforts. Their studies and many others, which have resulted in cooperative learning being the most closely examined development in education in this century, have concluded that students who work in cooperative classrooms learn more, remember the information longer, improve thinking skills, develop enhanced self-esteem, are more tolerant of individual and cultural differences, and are genuinely nicer to each other.

Cooperative Learning Strategies

Pairs

I used a number of cooperative learning strategies and group structures with my students. Some strategies were quick and informal and used student-chosen groups. These were usually pair strategies, which I used to focus attention during lectures or whole-class formal discussions. Onc pair strategy is *turn to your neighbor and . . . .* I would say to kids, "Pick someone who is sitting near you to be your neighbor for this discussion. Slide your desks close together. Whenever I say, 'Turn to your neighbor and . . . ,' the two of you will have approximately one minute to buzz about your thoughts. I will then randomly call on pairs to share their thoughts with the rest of the class."

Maybe we were studying gases and their behavior. I'd hold up a partially inflated balloon and say, "I'm going to put this balloon into that pot of boiling water. But before I do, turn to your neighbor and buzz about what you think will happen to the size of the balloon when the air inside is heated. Will the balloon get larger, smaller, or stay the same size?"

The kids would buzz for a moment. I would signal for silence, call on a few pairs for answers, and then we'd move on. I would put the balloon in the hot water, we'd see what actually happened, and then I might ask, "What do you think the change in the size of the balloon tells us about changes in the movements of the air molecules in the balloon? Turn to your neighbor and buzz about it." After the buzzing, a few pairs would again be asked to share their answers with the class.

A more formal way to pair, and one that might be more helpful when students need to do some higher level thinking, is *think, pair, share.* Students again pick a partner and slide their desks close together. The teacher asks a question, and then says, "Think." Students have anywhere from a few seconds to a minute or two to silently and individually think of some answers. The teacher may suggest that students try to think of at least three answers. I also suggested that students write down their individual answers. When the think time is over, the teacher says, "Pair. Trade answers with your partner." Student pairs may be asked to agree on their best answer or develop a list of many answers. When it is time to "Share," the teacher may ask pairs to volunteer their answers or may call on pairs for answers. The teacher will probably also want to record those shared answers on chart paper or on the blackboard.

The social skills I built into either of these quick, informal pair strategies focused on acceptance of others' ideas and encouraging others. I also asked my students to follow the *LEARN* guidelines. I told them that when we brainstorm, we

Look for original ideas

Energize each other

Accept each other's ideas

Rotate speakers

Note numerous ideas.

I introduced these guidelines to students before the first pair activity and had the guidelines posted on the wall so we could always refer to them. I found that they worked well to promote a courteous interchange of ideas, both in the pairs and in whole-class discussions.

1. Ask students to pick partners, move their seats close together so that they can work together, and tell each other one reason they feel glad that they can do this activity with a partner. Then say, "I often ask you to do things in teams in this class. I ask you to work with a partner or as a member of a small group. Today I want to focus on the actions you can take and the thinking you can do to help that teamwork be effective."

2. "We're going to start a KWL about teamwork." (If you want to call it cooperative learning, that's fine, too. Because teamwork is a lifelong skill, I like to use that term.)

3. Ask students to review what KWL means. Then say, "With your partner, please brainstorm five thoughts you have about effective, helpful teamwork and five pieces of knowledge you want to learn to enhance the quality of your teamwork. Each pair— five Ks and five Ws." Ask a volunteer to paraphrase the instructions. Then ask students to begin the KWL.

4. Give the pairs five to ten minutes to do their work. Then ask each pair to join another pair and trade ideas. In the foursome, one person is the conductor, who keeps the group focused, on task, and on time. A second person is the scribe, who records the official group copy of the work and reports to the rest of the class. A third person is the questioner, who checks for agreement and understanding. The fourth member of the group is

the host, who encourages everyone to participate and listen to others. Give the groups of four some time to develop a list of Ks and Ws.

5. Next do a wraparound to collect the Ks and Ws from the groups. Record them on a sheet of newsprint so that you and the class can periodically look over the list, correct any Ks that were incomplete or inaccurate, check off Ws, add new Ws, and add Ls. When students are part of the team building process, they feel capable and empowered and the team building is enhanced.

6. Ask groups to self-evaluate by answering these questions: How did doing the KWL help us clarify our thinking about teamwork. What did we remember that we sometimes lose sight of? What do we want to learn first? What was strong about our teamwork? What do we want to strengthen next time?

7. Ask teams to celebrate success. ◆

Short-Term Task Groups

Sometimes I wanted to use groups of three to five students for short periods of time—maybe for one or two class periods. If students had little experience with cooperative learning, I found that I needed to monitor these larger groups very closely to facilitate smooth functioning. (I do not recommend that students work in groups of more than five unless they are very skilled in cooperative learning. Even the most skilled students work best in groups of no more than three most of the time.) I randomly assigned students to these groups. I might ask them to number off from one to eight if I wanted eight groups. I might use paper slips of three different colors (e.g., green, pink, and brown), hand each student a slip of paper, and say, "Please form groups that contain one green, one pink, and one brown 'person.'" I might use playing cards, give each student a playing card, and then say, "Threes are a group, fours are a group, and so on."

I would tell the kids, "One of my goals is to give you an opportunity to work with every other student in this class at least once. Please work with your 'assigned' group today so that you have a chance to work with new people and learn from them." I asked these randomly assigned groups to do a content learning task together. Often the task involved repetitions of the same basic task with different examples—for example, building models of different molecules, doing balanced equations with colored magnets on pizza pans, or "counting by weighing" using different objects. Each member of the group was to do a single part of the task, explaining out loud what he was doing and why he was doing it "his way" as he did his part. Others were to ask clarifying questions or paraphrase what was said. The explaining, questioning, and paraphrasing really helped students learn the skills better and remember them longer.

Base Teams

My base teams were long-term teams and usually contained three or four students. I didn't assign students to base teams until I had a chance to collect information about their prior academic achievement. I asked them, "Look back on your grades from seventh grade until now and tell me your average science grade? math grade? English grade?" I also asked, "How do you think you learn best—by reading and writing, doing, watching videos, drawing, using mnemonics, or singing?" I watched them as they worked in pairs and in the short-term task groups. When I believed that I could do a reasonable job of assigning kids to heterogeneous base teams that mixed gender, ethnic origin, achievement, and multiple intelligence comfort zones (explained in Chapter 6), I set up the base teams. I told kids that there were reasons for the way I assigned the teams. I told them that I thought they could work together successfully. I said, "I do not expect you to become best friends. But I do expect you to work together politely, pleasantly, and professionally."

The base teams worked on major projects and presentations. Members told each other what work they had missed when they were absent and helped with make-up work. They helped each other set personal goals and concurrently evaluated goal achievement. They stayed together for at least one quarter of the school year.

Students did much of their best work in base teams. Members of base teams often became very good friends and spent time outside of school doing nonacademic things like having pizza parties or renting and watching movies together.

Making Cooperative Learning Work

Whether we were doing a quick pair activity or a longer team activity, we started every teamwork session with a trust-building activity. Sometimes the activity was short and snappy—"Lean in and tell your partner or group what time you went to sleep last night (or what you ate before you came to school this morning, your favorite new song, a pet you would like to have)." Some trust builders took a little more time—"What's a place in the world you would like to see and why? Describe a 'dream' day away from school. What's your favorite athletic activity and why? If you could be in a TV show, which one would you like to be in and why?"

Base team members picked team names (related to a given content theme), designed team flags, and practiced team energizers and celebrations. The trust-building activities enhanced the teamwork. They gave kids a chance to learn a little bit more about each other. Often, they learned that they had more in common than they realized. Students who trust each other work together more cooperatively, produce better work, and learn more.

1. Ask each student to think of her favorite kind of weather and the visual images that influence her choice. Then assign students to groups of three. One member of the group is the artist, who designs the final graphic and keeps the group focused, on task, and on time. A second person is the calligrapher, who does any necessary lettering and checks to be sure that everyone understands the work and that the group has reached consensus. The third member of the group is the colorizer, who colors the drawings and encourages group members to listen to each other, use encouraging words only, and celebrate success.

2. Each student will share her weather choice and reasons for liking that kind of weather with members of the group. The group will then discuss their weather likes and dislikes and reach consensus on a kind of weather that the group would be satisfied with. Stress that this is not necessarily any one person's favorite kind of weather. It is a weather pattern that everyone in the group would be willing to live with. The group is then to design and draw a graphic illustrating themselves experiencing that weather.

3. After the groups have done their graphics, ask them to share their drawings with the rest of the class. Display the finished graphics on the wall of the room to celebrate success. Ask groups to self-evaluate by answering these questions: What did we learn about trust-building activities? What did we learn about the process of reaching consensus? What did we do well as a team? What would we like to improve next time? ◆

Developing Social Skills

Every time students worked in cooperative teams, I asked them to be aware of what they did and said and to practice using positive, polite, responsible behaviors. Their focus on using these behaviors—behaviors that David and Roger Johnson identify as positive social skills—helped us to maintain the climate for quality in the classroom.

Several lists of social skills exist. Most of these categorize behaviors as simple, intermediate, or complex. Some simple skills include getting into groups quickly and quietly, standing or sitting knee-to-knee and eye-to-eye, and staying together mentally and physically. Mid-level skills include interactive listening, encouraging, paraphrasing each others' ideas, and inviting participation from everyone in the group. High-level skills include disagreeing with ideas rather than people, seeking and accepting differences, integrating different ideas or points of view, and seeking and reaching consensus. I encouraged kids to learn and do the simple skills very quickly.

Accepting Differences. Along with the simple skills, we focused on a few more complex skills during the course of the year. The first was accepting differences. From the first day of school I modeled this by letting kids know that I expected us all to have different pictures of an ideal classroom and to see and hear things differently. I told them, "Different does not mean wrong—it means different. Sometimes there is one right answer or idea, such as in some science content. At other times, in any subject, we can have different ideas. I expect that. We are thirty different control systems seeing the world through thirty different sets of filters."

I taught them to tug at ideas, not people, by learning to say things like, "I think you said you prefer plastic grocery bags. Is that what you said?" or "I heard you say you prefer plastic grocery bags. I prefer paper because it comes from a renewable resource" or "I see clear-cut forest when I see paper grocery bags. What do you see?" In teaching them this kind of interaction, I stressed using value-neutral vocabulary. I encouraged them to say, "You prefer plastic" not "You think plastic is good." I asked them to practice saying, "I prefer paper" not "I think plastic is bad."

I asked them to be aware of how their voices sound as they talk. I suggested that trouble can start when people use a dismissive or sarcastic tone of voice.

As we practiced accepting different points of view, we also learned to tug at ideas, not people. I encouraged students to avoid saying things like, "Why do you like plastic? That's dumb!" To me, expecting and accepting differences and tugging at ideas rather than people go hand in hand. They are key skills for students to learn in a quality classroom.

Being Good Listeners. I asked students to become good, inter-active listeners. Most students or adults who feel powerless have no one who really listens to them. When we are listened to, we feel that our worth and the worth of our ideas is being recognized; we feel good about ourselves. We feel that we have the ability to communicate effectively with someone else. Being listened to is the single most empowering activity we can experience. I believe that helping students develop listening skills helps them become need-fulfilling to each other, and that if they are need-fulfilling to each other, they are more likely to include each other and the class in their quality worlds.

Encouraging Others. One final social skill that I strongly urged students to use from the first day of school on was encouraging. I said, "This classroom is our *Home on the Range.* We will not hear discouraging words here because they will not be used. That includes teasing. I know that we all think teasing doesn't hurt because we only tease our friends and they will know that we're only teasing, but sometimes people don't feel like being teased and sometimes our teasing is something that even friends don't like—they may not tell us just how much they dislike the teasing because they don't want to 'rock the boat.' I will talk to you the way I'm asking you to talk to each other and me."

We talked about the importance of simple things like saying hello and goodbye to each other, smiling when we meet, and focusing on neutral or positive language. We worked on celebrating success together using cheers and other energizers. I felt the difference in the classroom atmosphere as teasing and discouraging disappeared. I found ways to remind students to encourage each other without saying, "Encourage each other." One of my favorite tactics was to say, "I see some buffalo roaming in here today," or "I sure wish I could see a few more deer and antelope playing in here today." The kids picked up on these verbal cues very quickly.

I know that some cooperative learning programs place very little emphasis on teaching and emphasizing the use of positive social skills. I also know that teachers who have done cooperative learning both ways report to me that students bond better, develop more trust, do better work, construct better products, and like class more when social skills are explicitly taught and modeled. The focus on polite behavior reinforces the climate for developing cooperation, building higher-level thinking, and doing quality work.

1. Ask students, "Is encouraging the same thing as praising? Are there differences in what we say and what we do when we praise and when we encourage? Take some time to think about an answer."

2. While students are thinking about the answer, move them into groups of three. One member of the group is the conductor, who keeps the group focused, on task, and on time. A second member is the editor, who writes down the group copy of the assignment and reports to the rest of the class. The third group member is the referee, who encourages everyone to participate and to use encouraging words only.

3. Tell students, "Your job is to brainstorm a list of things that people say and do to encourage each other. Don't worry about whether a comment or action is encouraging or praising at first. Remember the LEARN guidelines—we want lots of ideas. Take three minutes to brainstorm the list."

4. When groups are done brainstorming, say, "Now go back through the list and decide whether comments and actions are encouraging or praising. Label them with an E or a P." Groups will need ten to fifteen minutes to do the sorting—to discuss and reach consensus.

5. Finally, do a wraparound to collect encouraging ideas from the entire class. Post the list in the room and ask, "Are these things that we are willing to say and do with each other? Do we want to encourage each other?" Caution students about praise. Often praise sounds like external evaluation and can weaken an individual. Encourage students to give themselves credit for doing something well and to self-evaluate so that they know when they have done a quality job. ◆

Processing Social Skills

When students process their learning and behaviors regularly, they also learn more, integrate new learning with old better, develop more effective thinking skills, produce higher quality work, and develop social skills faster. I asked kids to do some processing every day by writing journal entries that answered the questions, What's one new thing I learned today (or one prior learning I rediscovered) about course content or effective behavior? How does this learning apply outside of this classroom? What was my best *doing* behavior? How can I improve what I do?

If cooperative groups were finishing an activity, I asked them to write group answers to these or similar questions. Group journals were kept in group folders in the classroom. I also asked cooperative groups to focus on specific social skills when they processed. I asked questions like, "What was our best encouraging behavior? How can we become better encouragers?" or "What did we say to show that we accept differences? What else could we say?"

Sometimes we did even quicker processing. I might ask, "What signal would you give your overall doing today—thumbs up, thumbs sideways, or thumbs down—and why did you choose that signal?" or "Draw a face that expresses your thinking and feeling about your doing today—smiley face, so-so face, or frowny face. Write down your reasons for picking the face you drew." Other examples include, "If today were a color, it would be_____ because . . . ." and "If today were a musical instrument, it would be_____ because . . . ."

I asked students to write thank you notes about helpful behaviors to their teammates. A lead-in might be, "Thank you for doing _____ today. Your action helped me because _____." Whatever strategy I used, I always had students do some processing before they left the classroom.

Self-evaluation is one of the most powerful tools we can give students for improving quality, and daily processing is part of that self-evaluation. The Johnson and Johnson cooperative learning model stresses the importance of frequent individual and team processing. Other models do not. Teachers who have tried doing cooperative learning with and without processing have told me that students show more growth faster when they process. I saw that for myself.

When I first started using cooperative learning, I frequently heard the bell ring at the end of class before I had asked students to do any processing. Rather than doing the processing at the start of the next class period, I just did not have them do it. I told myself that students in my classes had always done good work without processing, and that I could expect the same good work, processing or not. I used the common excuse that I did not have time for processing or I ran out of time before we could process.

As I became a better time manager and began to include processing more and more often, I found out how wrong I had been. Processing gives students a metacognitive moment to reflect on the learning and teamwork strategies they used, analyze the effectiveness of those strategies, and plan for improvement. It encourages them to evaluate the effectiveness of their behaviors and to choose or learn more effective behaviors. The added awareness of what they are doing and how it works helps students become more intentional in their use of effective behaviors. Their intentionality leads to higher quality learning and an enhanced classroom climate.

The Results of Cooperative Learning

I knew from personal observation that cooperative learning was successful. I learned why when I studied choice theory. Cooperative learning classrooms are very need-satisfying places. Students who work in a cooperative classroom believe they have a better chance of surviving academically. One of my hardest "sells" during my first year of cooperative learning involved a student who was a very high achiever, who always worked by himself, and who was very competitive. During the third quarter of the year, a newspaper reporter asked if she could visit the class he was in to talk with some of the kids about their perceptions of cooperative learning. I realized how well cooperative learning had sold itself when I heard this student telling her, "I didn't want to work in groups at first. I didn't see how these other kids could help me. I always got the best grades in classes when I worked by myself. What I'm finding is that by teaching these other kids and having them explain it back to me, I remember what I've learned a lot longer. Also, the teacher sometimes gives us assignments that include drawing pictures or singing songs or acting something out. I've found that these assignments help me learn, but other kids have better ideas for how to do them than I do. I can help more with the math and the writing. They can help me draw, act, and sing."

Other students who had not experienced the high learning and grades that this boy had came into class with low achievement expectations. These kids found that they were more successful than they had thought possible. They lost much of their anxiety about being in a science classroom when they realized that cooperative learning would help them survive academically.

Cooperative learning teams help students feel connected to the classroom. Because students are encouraged to use respectful, responsible behavior toward one another, they feel accepted in the classroom. This feeling of respect and belonging helps promote self-esteem, and it helps students satisfy their need for belonging. This is particularly true for special needs students. Special education and ESL teachers have told me that cooperative learning teams give the kids in their programs built-in resource groups in a potentially difficult course.

Students have some choices—some freedom—when they are working in a cooperative classroom. They can choose who has which role in the group, the pace at which they work, and sometimes what the final group product will be. Students working in cooperative teams practice listening to each other, which is very empowering. Students like to work together. In the course of their work they tell jokes, they laugh at each other's comments, and they feel a sense of wonder at what they are learning. They feel good about their mutual achievement.

A cooperative classroom helps students satisfy all five basic needs. It becomes a classroom in which they can feel successful, so they want to be there. It is a classroom in which everyone treats everyone else with respect and consideration, so coercion disappears. It is a classroom in which students frequently self-evaluate, individually and in groups, and it is, therefore, a classroom in which students continuously seek to improve their performance and their products. Cooperative learning is one of the most need-satisfying strategies that a teacher can use.

Using cooperative learning well takes practice. Teachers can practice using cooperative strategies as they work on school-improvement committees, and they can use many small, simple lessons with students to gain comfort and skill. Planning effective cooperative lessons can take a lot of time. Teachers may wonder just exactly what they are getting for their commitment of time. My answer is that establishing a cooperative classroom is of vital importance when a teacher is trying to build a quality classroom.

CHAPTER

6

Testing the Steering

Multiple Intelligences

I'm in my car and ready to go—almost. I want to check the steering wheel to be sure it's set for me. Is the tilt right? Is the seat too close or too far away? When I put the car in gear and step on the accelerator, will I feel comfortable and in control? I need to have the steering set right in order to drive with confidence. When we ask kids to learn in the classroom, do they have a chance to steer comfortably at least some of the time? Do we target different intelligences when we plan lessons so that each kid can work in a personal comfort zone some of the time? Do we structure activities so that kids can strengthen areas of less comfort? Do we give intelligences a chance to develop? Do we let kids experience a state of flow—a state of comfortable challenge? If all of the lessons target only the teacher's intelligence comfort zones, some of the kids will probably never be comfortable with their classroom driving.

TARGETING MULTIPLE INTELLIGENCES

Looks Like	Sounds Like
• lots of "kid art" on the walls	• "What color is your day?"
• varied equipment: video camera, tape recorder, radio, big paper, markers, manipulatives	• singing or rhythmic reciting
• lots of books and writing samples in the room	• kids and teacher reading out loud
• kids and teacher writing in journals	• background music playing
• kids working in cooperative groups	• buzz of voices
• kids doing pantomime or other "acting out" learning	• "Move like a cold molecule."

Figure 6.1

When I started using the Johnson and Johnson cooperative learning model in the classroom, I also started using Howard Gardner's theory of multiple intelligences. (Although I did not know the theory at the time, I think that my cooperative learning teachers did.) During my cooperative learning training I discovered that, as a student, I was more comfortable in a classroom when I could get up and move around, keep a personal journal, spend some time in individual reflection, do some of my learning as a member of a small group, and demonstrate what I had learned graphically, musically, and kinesthetically. When I transferred what I had learned in that cooperative learning training into my own classroom, I modeled the model by which I had learned. I saw that students became eagerly engaged in the classroom, happy to get there, sometimes reluctant to leave, and in control of their behaviors. I had never had many classroom "discipline problems," but a few students occasionally used disruptive behaviors. That began to happen less and less often, and students tended to self-correct when their behaviors were not responsible.

I explain this shift to more responsible behavior in choice theory terms—the cooperative, multiple intelligences classroom was a need-satisfying place for students. I discovered that other teachers who had undergone cooperative learning training with me were not experiencing quite the same success that I was. As we compared notes, I decided that the biggest difference between us was that they were not doing the musical, graphic, and kinesthetic activities that we had modeled in the training.

What I have since learned about Howard Gardner's theory of multiple intelligences helps me better explain the differences between our levels of success. I used lessons in the classroom that targeted each of Gardner's original seven identified intelligences. I gave kids an opportunity to show how they were word-smart, math-smart, body-smart, people-smart, picture-smart, music-smart, or self-smart. In doing so, I gave kids an opportunity to work in their personal comfort zone at least some of the time. The rest of the time they were willing to work in zones that were less comfortable. Targeting a given intelligence in a specific lesson was, for me, a matter asking myself, "What kinds of products would kids make if this were the targeted intelligence? Would that kind of product be appropriate for the content learning in the lesson? How can I structure the lesson to target the intelligence?" I did not force an intelligence to fit where the fit seemed awkward. I did try to target each intelligence for at least two major lessons each quarter.

The Theory and Development of Multiple Intelligences

Howard Gardner defines intelligence as a biophysical potential to recognize or identify problems and to invent solutions to problems or make products that are important within a particular cultural or community context. In his book *Frames of Mind,* published in 1983, Gardner proposed that we all possess at least seven intelligences. He rejected the theory that we have a single intelligence which can be measured with a single pencil-and-paper test that is administered outside of the regularly experienced learning environment. He argued that the standard intelligence tests that schools use actually measure (and, therefore, validate) only two of the seven intelligences—logical/mathematical and verbal/linguistic.

According to Gardner, in addition to those two, each of us has at least five more: visual/spatial, interpersonal/social, bodily/kinesthetic, musical/rhythmic, and intrapersonal/introspective. He has since identified an eighth, naturalist. Each of us possesses our own unique, ever changing blend of these intelligences. Because the blend is ever changing, an "intelligence inventory" that identifies an individual's strengths and weaknesses is meaningless over the long term.

When I have taught classes about Gardner's theory, participants occasionally commented about this. They said things like, "When I think about myself as a high school student, I think I was weak in math smarts. Now I think logical/mathematical intelligence is one of my areas of strength." My answer is, "Every day each of us has a new intelligence blend. As comfort in math increases, comfort in another intelligence may decrease. We may feel more comfortable in all the intelligences as we mature. Intelligence isn't static. We can always grow new brain-cell connectors—new dendrites."

1. Give each student a blank white sheet of paper. Ask them to set up axes for a bar graph:

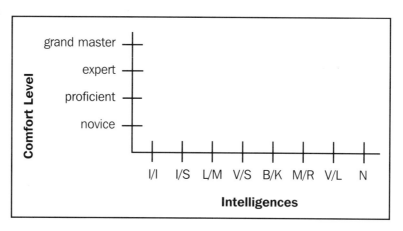

2. Tell the students, "I will describe some of the activities that target each of the intelligences. After you hear about an intelligence, I want you to draw a bar on the graph that you believe shows your comfort level with that intelligence."

3. As you read the descriptions, write them on the blackboard or on chart paper. Read the activities for the *intrapersonal/ introspective* intelligence; then ask for questions. Do the same for each of the other intelligences.

4. When you have finished, ask students to write a journal entry answering these questions: What did you learn by doing your

intelligence profile for today? Did any of your comfort zones surprise you? Which intelligences did you think would be your strongest comfort zones? Describe your thoughts about this statement: Don't ask me how smart I am; ask me how I am smart. Discuss your last answer with a neighbor.

5. After students have had time for sharing with a neighbor, ask for volunteers to share their last answers with the whole class. This can lead to a really exciting discussion.

Intelligences and Activities

Intrapersonal/Introspective: independent study, individualized activities, connecting learning to personal life, journaling

Interpersonal/Social: team learning, peer coaching, role plays, clubs and team sports, socializing

Logical/Mathematical: brain teasers, science experiments, comparing and contrasting, graphing, ranking, problem solving

Visual/Spatial: drawing, graphic organizers, color coding, visualizing, diagraming, developing metaphors

Bodily/Kinesthetic: hands-on (manipulatives), building or assembling, doing a sport, dancing, exercising, "acting out" an idea

Musical/Rhythmic: singing, writing song lyrics, poetry, rapping, listening to music, performing, playing an instrument, composing

Verbal/Linguistic: reading, writing, listening to lectures, discussing, story telling, joking and punning

Naturalist: sorting, categorizing, observing with the senses, planting and growing, investigating ecosystems or individual species or geology in the field, exploring conservation cycles ◆

The Role of Genetics

We can all develop each intelligence to a level of adequate competency. How far we develop in an intelligence depends on at least three factors. The first is individual genetics. One of my personal areas of strength is visualization. I can drive down a road from point

A to point B and have, in my brain, a bird's-eye-view of how I got there—much like a NASA photograph that includes roads, rivers, and other topographical information. I can drive from point B back to point A using a different route and add that information to my mental picture. And I can use the new route to go from A to B just as easily as I can use the original route—I just follow my mental map. I read printed maps easily and quickly. My mother has similar imaging and map-reading abilities. I believe that my strength in this area is due to a genetically inherited intelligence.

The Role of Encouragement and Training

The second factor that influences the development of an intelligence is the encouragement and training we receive in using that intelligence as we mature. Both of my parents encouraged my use of visualization skills. My mother, in addition to encouraging me to develop mental maps, would give me a small swatch of wallpaper, tell me to prop it up next to a wall, and say, "Now picture the whole wall papered in that pattern." When we were packing the car for a family vacation, my dad would say, "Look at the space we need to fill and pick out the suitcase or box that will fit." On the other hand, neither my school teachers nor my parents gave me much instruction in drawing and so, to this day, I draw only with much effort and then not very well. I believe that I could strengthen this aspect of my visual intelligence with practice.

The Role of Cultural Significance

The third factor involved in the development of an intelligence is the cultural importance that is placed on it or historical developments that were facilitated by its use. Mapmaking has been important to mankind as long as we have wandered from place to place in search of food. If the hunting or gathering was good in a particular spot, our ancestors wanted to be able to get back there again, and their pre-historic maps still exist as petroglyphs on cliff walls and in caves. Lewis and Clark mapped the course of their great voyage of discovery so that others could follow in their footsteps, take over the fur trade, and eventually establish a continental nation. Accurate outlines of land masses on naval maps were important to voyagers, who used coastal landmarks to get their bearings.

As a society of travelers and frontier-seekers, we valued our maps. Even when our traveling became more recreational, we used maps to help us find our way without wandering too far off course. My mental mapmaking abilities were encouraged by my family, valued by society at large, and encoded as one of my genetic abilities. All three factors worked together to influence my development of this intelligence. I am never lost. My mental maps get me where I want to go whenever I want to go there.

I have a friend who is very good at other kinds of visualization but who often gets lost. She can paint and draw pictures very well. She and I both have some talent in interior decorating, and we both enjoy looking at natural landscapes. We share some adequacies and also have individual strengths within the same intelligence—the visual/spatial intelligence.

Our intelligences do not usually operate independently from one another. Each activity we undertake involves a complex interaction of intelligences. If I want to drive from point A to point B, I visualize the route. I bodily/kinesthetically steer the car and work the gas and brake pedals and turn signals. I intrapersonally check my driving effectiveness; I remind myself to check the rearview mirror, to signal turns, to step on the brake in enough time to stop. I may not be aware of those reminders, but I make them all the same. I musically listen to a favorite radio station or tape recording while I drive to help the time pass faster. When I am driving in the city, I interpersonally remember that other drivers may be impatient or overtired, and I drive to stay out of their way.

As I write, I kinesthetically press the keys on my computer keyboard, intrapersonally reflect on where a piece is going next, verbally make vocabulary choices and syntax decisions, and mathematically number the pages. Everything I do represents using many intelligences. As I reflect on any waking activity, I can analyze it in terms of these main points of Gardner's theory: I possess all the intelligences; some intelligences are stronger than others and the blend is constantly changing; I have become at least adequately developed in all of them; my way of being competent in an intelligence is not the only way—there are many ways to be competent in every intelligence; everything I do uses many intelligences working together in interdependent, subtle ways.

Multiple Intelligences in the Classroom

As a classroom teacher, I wanted to remember these points whenever I planned lessons, activities, and assessments. I wanted to give all students an opportunity to work in intelligence areas of comfort some of the time. I also wanted all students to work in areas of discomfort part of the time. I wanted to encourage them to individually strengthen all of their intelligences, and to give them opportunities to work with other students who could help them become more comfortable and more competent in all the intelligences.

The Intrapersonal/Introspective Intelligence

I asked my students to use their intrapersonal/introspective intelligence in ways that many of them found uncomfortable, at least initially. Many of my students would have described themselves as "average" science students. While they were not really high achievers, they were not extremely low achievers either. They were just there in the middle somewhere. They did not know what their strengths or weaknesses were, mainly because they had not thought about analyzing their learning behaviors for effectiveness. They felt uncomfortable about being asked to learn science content on their own—by using focused reading activities, for example. If they had trouble with an assignment or a chunk of content learning, they often did not know where to go for help, again because they had never really taken the time to think about it. If they did well on tests, they said they got lucky. If they did poorly, they said, "I stubbed." Success and failure were a matter of luck, not a matter of planning.

I had them self-evaluate and asked, "Think about what an A student does to learn chemistry. If you could watch that person learning, what would you see her doing? If she got stuck, what might you see and hear? Which of her behaviors do you use? Do you know what you do when you study successfully? Pay attention to what works and what doesn't. I can't tell you what to do; I don't see things through your filters. You are the only person who can figure this out for yourself."

I asked kids to begin each class period with a short journal entry describing what we had done during the previous class, what unanswered questions they had about that learning, and what they could do to maintain their focus in class that day. At the end of every class I asked students to write another journal entry describing an important learning from the class and how it could be used outside of class. I encouraged them to look at what they had learned about thinking, reasoning, problem solving, and interacting with each other as well as content learning when they wrote the "log-out." I asked students to self-evaluate their performance for the week; set a personal performance goal in content learning, thinking skill learning, teamwork learning, or effective behavior learning for the upcoming week; and write a plan for reaching that goal.

Students were initially very uncomfortable with self-evaluation, goal setting, and planning. They were not used to using their intrapersonal muscles. I told them that this was like developing any skill, and that they would feel more comfortable as they practiced using it. I also told them that this kind of self-evaluation could help them become more effective in all areas of their lives. I told them that people who wander through life never thinking about what they are doing and never evaluating what is working and what isn't are doomed to repeat the same mistakes over and over again and are likely to be successful only by accident. I asked, "Do you want to be successful often and on purpose? If you do, stick with self-evaluation."

As they did, success in class happened more and more often, and many students told me that they had begun to self-evaluate in other aspects of their life. They liked success. They liked feeling competent. Their self-esteem improved because their accomplishments helped them feel more capable. Developing intrapersonal competence added quality to their lives.

1. Give each student a blank white sheet of paper and several colored markers. Say, "I am going to ask you to do a graphic that will tell a friend more about you. The first thing that I am going to ask is that you believe that a birthday elf comes to your house on your birthday and fills a stocking with gifts that describe the *real* you—the you that may be hidden inside. Do you believe? I like that—now draw the stocking. On the outside of the stocking, write three adjectives that describe the outer you—the you that other people see. Illustrate at least one of these adjectives. Then write three adjectives that describe the gifts inside the stocking—the parts of you that other people may not see. I will be asking you to share your stocking with a neighbor. You may want to remember that when you work on the inside part." Show an example to clarify the instructions.

2. Give students about five minutes to do their personal birthday stockings. Then tell them, "Share your stocking with a neighbor. Ask your neighbor to give examples of how the adjectives describe him or her. Give your neighbor that information about yourself."

3. Ask students to do a journal entry describing what was easiest for them in doing this assignment and what was most difficult. Ask them, "Did you learn anything new about yourself by doing the birthday stocking? How can you use that information?"

4. Celebrate completion by singing the happy birthday song, "Happy Birthday to US." ◆

The Interpersonal/Social Intelligence

In Chapter 5, I described how I helped students practice using their interpersonal/social intelligence in a cooperative learning setting. I believe that cooperative learning helps students be interpersonal while working on a content task; practice leadership and conflict management skills through shared responsibilities and assigned roles; learn content at a ninety-five percent mastery level as they teach their teammates; and practice reading others' feelings from facial expressions and body language. A cooperative classroom gives them a safe-risk environment within which they can express empathy for others and reveal their own feelings. Cooperative activities provide a structured, positive way for kids to offer help to others. A cooperative classroom is a need-satisfying place where students develop more interpersonal competence. They experience increased self-esteem because they feel accepted, included, helpful, and capable.

The Logical/Mathematical Intelligence

The chemistry content that I taught provided me with lots of opportunities to help kids develop more logical/mathematical skill. They made measurements in lab that were used in calculating or graphing. They made qualitative observations that were used to sort substances into categories. They looked for the underlying causes of physical and chemical change in lab. They analyzed information from the text to find causes of real-world phenomena like the corrosion of the Statue of Liberty, the explosion of the Hindenburg, the expansion of weather balloons, or fish die-offs in the Columbia River.

I asked my students to make predictions about the impact of chemistry on industry. For example, I asked them to analyze the rate at which iron ore is being mined, compare the rate of mining with the estimated reserves of iron ore, and predict when recycling of iron will replace mining of ore as a source of "new" metal. We looked at chemical bonding and molecular shape in order to understand how substances get their properties—more cause and effect, this time at the molecular level.

I think that some logical/mathematical activities can be designed into *any* curricular content—we need to realize that "math smart" means more than working with numbers. Whenever we ask kids to analyze attributes, to predict and test those predictions, to sequence operations or to develop time lines, to prioritize or to use cause-and-effect reasoning, we are giving them an opportunity to use their logical/mathematical skills. Kids (and adults) of all ages can develop these skills. As they do, they will feel more capable as problem solvers and that they are in more effective control of their lives. Becoming competent in math smarts will add quality to their lives.

The Visual/Spatial Intelligence

When I received cooperative learning training, my teachers asked our class cooperative groups to produce visuals on large sheets of newsprint for use as teaching tools. I think that they also used the visuals to assess the accuracy of our learning. I found that producing visuals with colored markers—often using a graphic organizer like a mind map, a Venn diagram, or a grid—and combining words and colors with pictures enhanced my learning and that of my team-mates. I transferred the technique to my own classroom. Large sheets of paper and colored markers became standard equipment and I planned for at least one lesson per week to include some kind of visual/spatial activity.

Suddenly students who had been average achievers and some-what disengaged learners became eager, active ones. These were the kids who loved to draw and produce graphics and who, I discovered, learned best when they were asked to visualize and sketch. They became group leaders during visual activities. They became group "artists," lightly sketching pictures in pencil for their team-mates to color.

I began to ask students to produce mind maps instead of outlines to organize information. I asked them to do storyboards instead of essays to explain observed phenomena. I asked them to list the properties of a substance in pictures and words. I asked them to compare/contrast using Venn diagrams that combined words and pictures.

I frequently had students prepare for a group product project by doing an individual "rough draft" as homework. The groups could combine the best ideas from the individual rough drafts to create the final product. Groups recorded their products on large sheets of paper and presented their finished products to the class. We displayed finished products on the walls of the room. Students looked at and learned from each others' visual products.

I got a better understanding of their mental pictures of content information, and I was able to use that understanding to correct errors. Some students, for example, pictured molecules as actually swelling in size (rather than just moving farther apart and faster) when temperature increased. I asked students to "black out" incorrect pictures and draw correct ones. This correcting helped them develop new, accurate mental images of content learning.

As the year progressed and we did more and more visual work, students who were very uncomfortable using this intelligence became more comfortable. They were adding a new dimension to their learning, a dimension that uses the physical sense—seeing—and that gives those of us who are sighted most of our information about the world around us. Strengthening this link between information gathering and information processing helped students become better learners who experienced more success in the classroom. Their increased success strengthened their quality world pictures of the classroom.

The Bodily/Kinesthetic Intelligence

Asking students to produce and use graphics also made the classroom more comfortable for students who were strong bodily/kinesthetic learners. These are kids who learn best by doing and who love activities that involve movement. The physical movement required to produce graphics as well as the mental movement around the paper that kids experience as they work on them help the bodily/kinesthetic learners become more engaged in the classroom. These are also the kids who love manipulatives.

I always had a few manipulatives sitting in a "touch me" location on my desk near the classroom door. I put them in that location early in the school year, and told the kids they had permission to pick up anything they found sitting there without asking first. (We had already talked about why I wanted them to ask permission before picking up objects in a chemistry room, and the broader idea of respecting other people's property and handling property only with permission from the owner.) Some students walked past these objects every day and never touched them. Others picked them up and "played" with them almost every day without seeming to lose interest and would ask where a manipulative was when I replaced it with something else. I changed the manipulatives several times during the year.

I planned lessons that used puzzles, molecular models, balloons, styrofoam balls, and magnets to help kids learn content. Early in the year, I paid attention to who played with the things on my desk most often, and I tried to have one of these kids in each group whenever we worked with manipulatives.

1. To celebrate the successful completion of an assignment or other class work, ask the kids to stand. Then say, "We're going to do a cheer together, and instead of just yelling out the cheer, we're also going to act it out." Ask if they are familiar with the song *YMCA* and the way the letters are acted out in the song. Demonstrate for them.

2. Then say, "The cheer that we are going to do is 'Spell Quality.' Do you think you know how to do the letters? I'll demonstrate for you." Use your arms to form the letters as you say them. Repeat if the kids ask you to. Then lead them in the cheer. ◆

Kids who feel comfortable doing bodily/kinesthetic activities also loved doing lab work. They loved working with the equipment. They especially seemed to enjoy doing more complicated equipment set-ups and tear-downs. They also enjoyed acting out molecular motion in solids, liquids, and gases using arm motions to mimic bond movement, doing "square dances" that represented different types of chemical processes, and playing charades to review vocabulary words.

I suspect that some teachers may feel that science content "fits" bodily/kinesthetic learning easily, and that other subject-matter content is more difficult to adapt to bodily/kinesthetic activities. I know that laboratory activity is seen as a kinesthetic "natural." However, I believe that *all* teachers can find ways to include kinesthetic activities in their classrooms. Any content area can use graphic organizers. Teachers can find ways to use manipulatives like puzzles, blueprints or maps with movable markers, or modeling clay in any content area. Charades or pantomime can be used to introduce or review a wide variety of content learning. In addition, I believe that the bodily/kinesthetic learner will feel more comfortable in a classroom where she knows that she can get out of her seat to stretch or move around from time to time, as long as she does not disturb other students with her movement.

I was a kid who was asked by many teachers, "Can't you just sit still?" Although I tried very hard to do as they asked, I still found myself unconsciously kicking the back of the desk in front of me or sliding my desk into the one behind me after the admonition to sit still had worn off. Then one day a teacher asked me, "If I give you a seat in the back of the room so that you can stand up and stretch from time to time, do you think you can do that without disturbing the other students? Do you think you can be quiet about your stretching?" I promised that I would, and the strategy worked.

Finding ways to include bodily/kinesthetic learning activities and providing students with opportunities to relieve the pent-up physical need to move that some of them have will help them feel more competent and comfortable in the classroom, and this will, in turn, strengthen the quality world pictures of the classroom that they have developed and help them become more effective learners.

The Musical/Rhythmic Intelligence

Musical/rhythmic activities can add fun and excitement to the classroom while enhancing learning. In every class I always had several students who were very comfortable doing musical/rhythmic activities. They would come into the classroom humming or singing; they would tap out gentle rhythms with their pencils; they remembered snatches of poetry; they did little dance steps as they moved around the room; they noticed sounds from the hallway, rain or hail on the roof; or they seemed to hear the soundtrack from the movie in the next classroom more than other students did. I found many ways to identify these kids, and I assigned one to each group at the start of a musical/rhythmic activity. Each group had four or five members instead of the usual three. I knew that the kids who did not feel comfortable with this intelligence would feel less anxious if their group had at least one member liked to perform.

I asked kids to write song lyrics and then perform their songs in class. Many of the songs were written to the tunes of nursery rhymes like "The Farmer in the Dell," "Three Blind Mice," and "The Itsy Bitsy Spider." All the songs were rooted in content. The following, to the tune of "Twinkle, Twinkle Little Star," is one example.

> Water's freezing, watch it grow.
> It's expanding as you know.
> Bigger volume, same old weight—
> Lower density's its fate.
> This means ice will always float
> Like a little frozen boat.

IRI/SkyLight Training and Publishing, Inc.

Sometimes we did simple, two-line rhymes to help us remember frequently used facts:

> Red in acid, blue in base—
> Litmus colors for either case.
>
> You really, really oughter
> Put acid into water.

Activity 17

1. Show students the poem "Fog" by Carl Sandburg. Have a copy of the poem written on a large sheet of newsprint that is taped up on the front board or wall. Examine Sandburg's personification of the fog. Then show the class a second sheet of newsprint that has lots of blanks in place of the words in the original poem:

   The _____ _____ on _____
   _____ _____ and so on.

2. Tell students, "You will be working in groups to rewrite this poem to personify a quality classroom. One group will work on classroom climate. The other five will each do one of the five fingers. Your rewrite will be true to the spirit of the original poem." Ask for questions. Clarify the assignment.

3. Assign the students to form groups of four. Each group will need a conductor to keep the group on time and on task, a poet to write the group copy of the rewrite on chart paper, an orator to read the finished product to the rest of the class, and a manager, who reminds group members to use encouraging words only and encourages everyone to participate. Give groups twenty minutes to do the rewrite. Then do the poem presentations.

4. Ask groups to self-evaluate by answering these questions: What was the easiest part of doing this assignment? What was the hardest? How comfortable do we feel using the musical/rhythmic intelligence? How can we strengthen this comfort zone?

5. Celebrate success by doing the "Spell Quality" cheer (see Activity 16). ◆

I occasionally played soft music when students were working together in pairs or small groups. Sometimes I picked the music and sometimes I let students bring it in. I asked them to choose music that could be played softly enough not to overwhelm mental concentration on chemistry. If any member of the class said that the music was a distraction, I turned it off. If those who enjoyed working to music asked why I turned if off, I kindly asked them to remember that we are all different and that one of those differences is how comfortably we work while music is playing. I suggested that we can all work with or without music as we wish in the privacy of our own workplaces. But we would not play background music if classmates found it hurt their concentration.

I also encouraged students to make up mnemonics to help them memorize information. I asked, "Did any of you learn to spell the word 'arithmetic' by learning the sentence, 'A rat in the house might eat the ice cream?' I did! Your assignment is to make up a nonsense sentence that will help you remember the symbols of the first ten elements."

Students worked individually at first. Then they shared their sentences with members of their base teams. Finally, each base team shared its favorite sentence with the whole class. Students were encouraged to choose a sentence to remember. (Some former students have reported to me that years later they still remember the mnemonics they created.)

Students of all ages can write new lyrics to existing tunes, work to background music, create mnemonics, and write poems. Asking them to use their musical/rhythmic intelligence to learn science or math or social studies content gives students who are musically strong an opportunity to work in their comfort zones and, therefore, learn more effectively, do better quality work, and keep the picture of your classroom in their quality worlds.

The Verbal/Linguistic Intelligence

Verbal/linguistic intelligence is the last of the seven intelligences *originally* identified by Howard Gardner. I believe that every teacher in every classroom realizes that good reading and writing skills are vital to successful lifelong learning, and I believe that all classroom teachers can help students become better readers and writers. According to Dr. Art Costa, the careful and precise use of language is a habit that all intelligent people share. By helping students become better readers and writers, we encourage the development of that habit.

IRI/SkyLight Training and Publishing, Inc.

I asked my students to write a three- to five-paragraph essay every two weeks or so. I encouraged them to check the quality of their writing before turning it in by using the rubric discussed in Chapter 3. When I read their essays, I highlighted words that I thought could be replaced with more precise ones. I also asked students to do a little writing each day by doing log or journal entries at the beginning and end of the class period. To model the process and emphasize its value, I wrote when they wrote. I asked them to connect today to yesterday and this class to real life when they made their journal entries. I read at least three entries per student per quarter. At the end of each quarter, I asked them to review their journals and find evidence of improvement in their journaling habits. I also asked them to review their essays and find evidence of better writing quality in these longer pieces.

I reminded students that writing would help them learn to express their thoughts as precisely as possible. I told them that people who speak and write well are more successful at finding meaningful employment. I suggested that people who use language precisely are more likely to get what they want without hurting others because they use vocabulary that is less likely to offend.

Students who were reluctant writers at the beginning of the year became willing writers as they saw that they could learn to write proficiently. I reminded them that we will not all become artistic writers, just as we will not all become world-class athletes, famous painters, or professional musicians, but we could all become capable and precise expressive writers.

I also encouraged students to believe that they could read the course textbook and learn from the reading. By the time many students got to the classes that I taught, they were discouraged science readers. They had not learned to read science materials any differently than they read novels.

I used a couple of tools to focus their attention when they read. One was the KWL chart we used at the beginning of some units. I gave each student a personal copy of the Ks and Ws that we had brainstormed as a class. Then I would say something like, "Before you come to class tomorrow, please read pages 101–106. Find answers to at least two of our Ws and pencil them into the L column on your KWL sheet. Check at least two Ks for accuracy and be ready to tell us if we really did have the correct information—and be ready to give us the number of the page in the book where you found the information."

I asked students how they could remember the Ws as they read. They would suggest strategies like looking over the Ws after reading two paragraphs to see if the reading had given them any answers. By going back and forth between the Ws and the reading, they focused on finding information that they said was important to learn. Finding those answers was a quality world picture because they wanted those answers.

Sometimes I focused students' attention on a reading by giving them a predication guide. I wrote a list of statements about the reading and asked students to go through the list and record agreement or disagreement with each statement *before* doing the reading. I often asked them to do the agree/disagree prereading activity during the last few minutes of a class period. Then I said, "Before you come to class tomorrow, please read pages 131–143. Decide whether the author agrees or disagrees with the statements. Record the agreement and the page number. If the author disagrees with a statement, rewrite the statement so that it expresses agreement with the author. Again, record the number of the page where you got your information."

The next day we would go through the prediction guide. Members of base teams would check each others' answers, and teams would decide on consensus answers to the questions. Then I would call on randomly selected students to share their team's answer to a question with the whole class. By doing the team checking first, I found that students tended to correct any misunderstandings that teammates had before they were called on to share the answer with the whole class, and I believe that the discussion involved in reaching a consensus answer helped to enhance the content learning.

Figure 6.2 is a sample prediction guide. When I write a prediction guide, I keep the questions in the order in which the information is included in the text and I use the vocabulary of the text. I try to mix up the agrees and disagrees so that I do not create a predictable pattern. I include some statements that partially agree with the text and have the students rewrite these statements so they totally agree with the text.

Students found that prediction guides helped them learn as they read. Looking for specific information helped them maintain their concentration. Students told me that using focused reading tools helped them understand that the reading was purposeful and could be useful to them. KWL and prediction guides helped students believe that they could learn by doing content reading. These tools also helped all students strengthen their verbal/linguistic intelligence.

The Naturalist Intelligence

In 1995, Howard Gardner proposed an eighth way of knowing—the naturalist intelligence. A person who is "nature smart" learns from

SAMPLE PREDICTION GUIDE

Prediction Guide:
Sources of and Replacements for Metals

Write an "A" in the "Me" column if you agree with a statement *before* doing the assigned reading. Write a "D" if you disagree.

After you do the reading, write an "A" in the "Author" column if the author agrees with a statement. Include the number of the page where you found the information. Write a "D" and the page number if the author disagrees with a statement and rewrite it so that it agrees with the author.

Me	Author	Statement
		Our resource needs/demands are fairly constant.
		Copper is widely used because of its good electrical conductivity and because it is easily alloyed with other metals.
		Any source of ore can be profitably mined.
		The percentage of a metal is fairly constant in all of its ores.
		Copper, silver, and gold were discovered early in history because of their widespread abundance and high chemical reactivity.
		Recycling processes always lose some of the material being recycled.
		Modern ceramics are very hard, have very high melting points, and are quite malleable.
		Nature distributes metal resources very diffusely; use by people concentrates metal deposits.

Figure 6.2

the natural world around her. She observes shapes, colors, movements, odors, and sounds and is able to categorize, classify, and make predictions based on these observations. She recognizes animals, plants, and minerals from their shapes and colors. She can forecast weather from cloud shapes and wind and water behavior. She can identify animals from their tracks. She feels happiest and most productive when she can gather information about the natural world through her senses and use that information to interpret and explain the natural world. She is likely to "grow up" to be a field biologist like Jane Goodall, a horticulturist, a farmer, or a commercial fisherwoman.

I believe that my naturalist intelligence helps me feel very comfortable in the wilderness. I love woods, wide-open spaces, and large expanses of water. In the woods close to my home, I can identify the different kinds of trees and what animals have left tracks. I can do some general weather predicting based on the behavior of the birds that come to the feeding stations set up around my home and from changes in wave and cloud patterns over Lake Superior. I have chosen to live in an area with a very low population density. These are all behaviors that demonstrate comfort in using the naturalist intelligence.

Some people find it difficult to distinguish between the naturalist and the logical/mathematical intelligences. Howard Gardner explained it as "the difference between Darwin and Newton." These two scientists developed their best-known theories using two very different approaches.

Darwin gathered information about animal life using the senses of hearing and sight. He was particularly fascinated by differences in bill shape and function among species of finches in the Galapagos Islands, and recorded at least nine different finch feeding habits that he attributed to differences in bill length. He used observations of animal behavior to develop his theory of evolution and to write *Origin of Species.*

Newton began to think about the law of gravity as he observed free-falling objects. He suspected that their paths were elliptical, and proceeded to use the formulae for the ellipse and for circular acceleration to mathematically derive the Law of Universal Gravitation. He used the elliptical orbits of planets, worked out by Kepler, to show, again mathematically, that the motion of the planets fit his law of gravity.

Darwin developed and communicated his theory using sensory observations about animals. Newton used abstract mathematical formulae. Darwin's expression was naturalistic; Newton's was logical/mathematical.

As I reflected on my classroom lessons, I realized that some activities did ask students to use their naturalist intelligence. For example, after we had defined elements as being made up of a single kind of atom, compounds as composed of identical molecules that contained atoms of two or more elements, and mixtures as containing two or more kinds of molecules and/or atoms, I gave students small boxes of hardware pieces. Some boxes contained a single kind of hardware piece—one size and shape of nut or bolt or washer. Some contained identical combined pieces, such as several identical bolts, each with an individual nut screwed on. Some boxes were a hodgepodge of different kinds and sizes of nuts or bolts or washers thrown together at random. I asked the kids to look at the hardware in each box and tell me if the pieces represented an element, a compound, or a mixture. Their observations of shape, size, and type helped them make the classifications.

After we described the physical properties of metals and nonmetals, I put small samples of about three dozen elements in petri dishes and set up work stations, each of which included a sample of an element, an electrical conductivity tester, and a small hammer and chisel to test for brittleness, and asked the kids to decide whether each of the elements was a metal or a nonmetal. In addition to electrical conductivity and brittleness, students used general appearance criteria like color, shininess, and physical state in order to classify.

Earth science teachers at my school had students test properties and observe appearances of rock samples to sort them by type, or look at slides of different cloud formations to classify them and determine what kind of weather they usually indicate. Biology students and their teachers planted a flower bulb garden on the school grounds, identified and did population counts of different grasses in small prairie patches that still exist in town, used two-liter pop bottles to create balanced terrariums in which the plants never needed watering, and went to the sand dunes near Illinois Beach State Park to do species counts based on animal tracks. These activities all ask kids to use their naturalist intelligence as they learned.

Kids can also use their "nature smarts" outside the area of science. In math, students can gather population data about different species of trees, birds, or flowers near their homes. The information can be presented as bar graphs or used to calculate percentages. Geography studies can include information about flora and fauna and minerals. Kids can compare plant and animal distribution "then and now" as they study history, or they can learn about how people used wind, cloud, and water wave information to make weather predictions as they explored new continents. Home economics students can plant herb gardens. Automotive repair students can develop "field guides" to different kinds of cars. Any subject matter offers opportunities for kids to use their naturalist intelligence.

1. Give each student a piece of aluminum foil, which must be at least as long as the person's foot. Tell the students to put their pieces of foil on the floor and step on the foil hard enough to leave an impression of their shoes in the foil. Each student has now made a record of her or his individual "track."

2. Collect the pieces of foil from the left half of the room first, put them down, and then collect the pieces from the right half of the room. The number of students in each half *must* be the same—if there is an odd number of students in the class, add your own track to the half that has one less student track than the other. Give the tracks from the right half of the room to the students on the left side and vice versa. Switching groups of tracks like this means that no student will get her or his own track back. Each student from the left half of the class will get one track from the right half; each student from the right half will get one track from the left half.

3. Tell students, "Now your job is to find the person who made the track that you have. Stand up, move around, look at the track, look at shoes—and find the person who made the track." This part of the activity can get somewhat chaotic. Students will all eventually be able to match the track to the person.

4. Next, ask students to suggest ways to speed up the matching process. Elicit the suggestion that defining categories of shoes might help. Ask for categories, such as running shoes, walking shoes, boots, sandals, and "street" shoes; kids know the types of shoes they wear and will be able to provide several categories.

5. Finally, set up a collection station for each category of shoe. Ask students to put their tracks in the appropriate category. Assign students to groups of three or four, give each group three or four tracks from one category, and say, "Your final job is to devise a general symbol for the sole of the type of shoe represented by the sample tracks that I gave your group. The tracks may not all be identical—in fact there are probably individual differences. Different examples of one type of shoe will have similarities. Your symbol will show those similarities. Your group needs a conductor to keep the group focused and

on time, an illustrator to draw the generalized track, a naturalist to describe the track to the class, and a guide to encourage everyone to participate and to remind everyone to use encouraging words only." Give groups ten to fifteen minutes to develop their generalized track symbols. Then have the groups present their symbols.

6. Ask groups to self-evaluate by answering these questions: What did we learn about developing generalized symbols for categories in nature? Could we extend this activity to produce a "guide to types of shoes"? What are some examples of commercially available field guides? What did we do well as we worked together? What do we want to improve next time?

7. Celebrate success by encouraging everyone to stamp their feet in some rhythmic pattern very loudly. Demonstrate the pattern—then do the group stomp. ◆

Restructuring the classroom so that different lessons target different intelligences requires time, energy, and a willingness to take risks and experience discomfort. We tend to teach lessons in a way that reflects our own personal comfort zones. As we design lessons that target our personal *dis*comfort zones, we experience feelings that some of our students routinely have—feelings of doubt, uneasiness, and potential failure. We also learn that lessons that target the three most often neglected intelligences are not just fun-and-games, as some critics charge. Lessons that target the bodily/kinesthetic, musical/rhythmic, or visual/spatial intelligence can help students learn accurate, meaningful content. About one-third of our students are most at ease when working in these intelligences. They are at risk of being labeled attention deficit or hyperactive when, in fact, they are seldom given the opportunity to work in personally satisfying ways. As we give them opportunities to work in their most comfortable intelligences, we access their quality worlds and they become more willing to work in their less comfortable intelligences. As they strengthen all of their intelligences, they become more successful in school, the quality of their work improves, and their behavior becomes more effective and responsible. The classroom becomes a need-satisfying place for all students and the teacher. Incorporating every intelligence into the learning process is *crucial* to establishing a quality classroom.

Is My Driving Quality?

Assessment and Evaluation

When I need to renew my driver's license, I know that I could be asked to demonstrate how well I drive or know the rules of the road by taking a driving or a paper-and-pencil test. I pick up a copy of Rules of the Road *a few weeks before the renewal date to give myself a chance to review. I know that being familiar with the rules is a must for convincing the examiner that I am a safe driver. This external evaluation occurs once every three years. In between official tests, I self-evaluate my driving habits. A traffic officer may concurrently evaluate my driving. If the officer's evaluation is different from mine, I may wind up with a ticket. I know that I can maintain good driving skills only by self-evaluating as I drive. How can students improve the quality of their learning? How can teachers improve the quality of their facilitation and mediation? As both groups practice concurrent evaluation, self-evaluation, and planning to reach personal goals, the quality of the classroom increases.*

QUALITY ASSESSMENT AND EVALUATION

Looks Like	Sounds Like
• some individual paper-and-pencil tests	• very quiet testing environment
• retaking tests in cooperative groups	• quiet discussion of answers; checking for understanding
• teacher using observation checklists; students self-evaluate using the same checklists	• teacher and student discussing/comparing filled-out checklists
• graphic organizers, story boards, other student-produced visuals	• students discussing "team" versions of visuals
• teacher using rubrics to evaluate student work; students self-evaluating using the same rubrics	• student and teacher discussing/comparing rubric scoring
• student-written poetry	• students reading poems or singing "content" songs
• students doing a physical task or acting out content learning	• sounds that accompany physical tasks
• student portfolios	• teacher-student and student-student portfolio conferences
• students setting goals and planning for success	• students sharing goal evaluations with each other

Figure 7.1

IRI/SkyLight Training and Publishing, Inc.

Quality assessment and evaluation in a classroom includes use of observation checklists, journals, rubrics, performances and projects, traditional teacher-written and standardized tests, and concurrent evaluation. The most important feature of assessment and evaluation in a quality classroom is cooperative student and teacher involvement in both processes—genuine student self-evaluation and student-to-student or student-to-teacher concurrent evaluation. As long as the teacher is the only person who gathers information about student performance and learning (assessment) and decides how good or bad the performance and the learning are (evaluation), she or he will not have a quality classroom. The students may do some very good learning, and some of it may be quality learning, but the trusting climate that results in a quality classroom will not exist.

I came through a system where the classroom teacher was the sole evaluator of performance. I worked very hard, I did the best work that I could do, I knew that it was better than the work most of my classmates were doing, and I wanted top grades for my efforts. I remember how I felt emotionally and what my body told me when I received a poor evaluation—I felt under siege mentally and bruised physically. I chose to defend my work by saying things like, "Well, I did the best job that I could. You didn't give us enough time," or "You didn't really explain what you wanted us to do. How could we do the assignment right?" or "It's not fair to test us on stuff that's not in the book."

I wanted to do good work, and I wanted to receive As. The teacher decided whether or not I got those grades and told me how she evaluated my work. I was never asked if I thought that my work was my best or if I could think of ways to improve my learning habits. I was never told the grading standards before I began the work. I was never asked to discuss my evaluation of my work with a teacher. I never felt like a partner in the evaluation process. As a result, I believe that I became a fairly typical defensive, "reactive" student who did not really question whether or not I was doing my best work. I only cared about whether or not I got the grades that I wanted. I did not learn about or practice self-evaluation.

As a teacher I had to do a self-evaluation every year, required by contract. It consisted of filling out a copy of a standard evaluation checklist that the teachers' union and administration had agreed to use. I never felt that this self-evaluation had any meaning. I did not see it as a tool for growth. I was asked to check off "meets district standards," "needs improvement," or "needs immediate attention" for about twenty separate behaviors. I was asked to identify one or two behaviors that I wanted to improve during the following school year and bring the completed copy of the document to an evaluation conference with an administrator.

We rarely discussed the self-evaluation. The administrator would give me a copy of an external evaluation (done on a different form) to read, ask me to add any statements I wanted (expected to have objections to the external evaluation), and sign the document. We never discussed my personal improvement goals. The administration defined improvement goals for the entire staff for the following year. I was never asked to develop a plan for reaching my personal goals. I was never asked to look at the goals from the prior year and decide if I had made any improvement. I decided that self-evaluation was just another exercise designed to improve the appearance of the evaluation process. I discounted the usefulness of self-evaluation, and continued to practice my organized, defensive behaviors.

Assessment As a Tool for Growth and Development

When I participated in the basic and advanced intensive trainings offered by the William Glasser Institute, I finally began to understand how effective self-evaluation could be as a tool for growth and improvement. In fact, even before I finished the basic week, I had decided that the key to developing a quality classroom was to help students learn to self-evaluate the effectiveness of their learning behaviors and the quality of their learning, and to encourage them to set personal learning goals and then develop plans that they could use to reach those goals. I began asking students to write a weekly journal entry that focused on their personal goal for the week, a review of the plan they developed to reach the goal, the effectiveness of the plan, how the plan could be improved to produce more progress toward the goal, identification of people who they felt could help them reach their goal, and a description of the help that they wanted those people to give them. I asked students to pick a partner with whom they would share their weekly self-evaluation—someone who would co-verify that they had done the self-evaluation and planning and who would celebrate success with them.

At first I gave students time to complete the self-evaluation and planning process in class. As time went on, I asked students to start the weekly self-evaluation in class and finish it outside of class if they needed more time. Students began to see improved learning and grades resulting from their self-evaluation and planning, so they were willing to do this "homework." (A detailed description of this weekly self-evaluation, including goal setting and planning, can be found in Chapter 5 of *A Multiple Intelligences Road to a Quality Classroom.*)

98

Assessment As a Behavior Checklist

I also began to use concurrent evaluation of content learning, course work, and behaviors extensively. I used a number of behavior checklists to assess and evaluate students' behaviors as teammates and learners. I decided to give each student a copy of each checklist I used. I asked them to use the checklists to evaluate their own behaviors several times per grading period. We had checklists that suggested specific behaviors to promote effective learning, teamwork, production of individual work, and responsibility. I told students which type of behavior I wanted them to self-evaluate on any given day. Students used the checklists to identify their less effective behaviors when they developed their improvement plans. (Copies of many of these checklists and descriptions of their uses can be found in Chapter 6 of *A Multiple Intelligences Road to a Quality Classroom).*

Assessment As a Tool to Evaluate Products

The students and I used rubrics, like the writing rubric described in Chapter 3, to evaluate final products—pieces of writing, graphics, visuals, performances, and products of projects. Students received copies of the rubrics before they started the work. I asked students to suggest changes or clarifications in the rubrics before we used them. The rubrics gave us a commonly agreed-upon set of standards prior to starting each job. Students could compare their work in progress with the rubric for the job as often as they wanted.

These comparisons often resulted in revisions that improved the work. Students became more comfortable at taking risks and trying new ways to develop products because they knew they would not be criticized for making mistakes. They knew that I would not evaluate their work until they presented me with a finished product. I encouraged students to be reasonable and realistic when we determined due dates for those products. We discussed the importance of being flexible. We decided that deadlines would be extended if more time was needed to insure quality products, or shortened if we found that creating a quality product took less time than we originally believed. The students and I discovered that our evaluations of the final products were usually in agreement.

We believed that establishing a rubric *before* students started a job was the secret to that agreement. Students learned that ongoing self-evaluation using standards that defined a quality product could help them do better work. Their acceptance of self-evaluation as a tool for improvement and growth helped them develop strong quality world pictures of self-evaluation as a valued behavior.

Assessment As a Tool to Check Content Mastery

Early in each content unit I would give students a list of concepts or skills that they would be asked to learn, which included an explanation of how those concepts or skills connected with the world outside of the classroom. Late in the unit we would review the list and I would ask them if they wanted to add any concepts or skills.

I asked students to demonstrate their learning in a variety of ways. At least three times per grading period, usually at the end of a content unit, students did individual assessment activities. Sometimes they took traditional pencil-and-paper tests. I explained that they would need to know how to perform well on such tests in future academic work, so I was trying to help them maintain or improve a skill that would be needed for future success. Sometimes students did individual writing, visuals, poems, calculations, graphs, or other products that demonstrated their content learning and then individually discussed that learning with me or with another student.

Students who believed that they had mastered the content were encouraged to "show-and-tell" me what they had learned. Those who demonstrated at least ninety-five percent content mastery were designated as experts. Students who were ready for show-and-tell after the experts had been tested could choose to demonstrate their learning to me or to one of the experts. Students who had not learned the material at a ninety-five percent level when they first chose to show-and-tell had two more chances to get to that level. The experts were honest and reliable when testing their classmates and reporting their scores. They felt that to be otherwise would be to betray a trust and jeopardize concurrent evaluation testing, a testing method that all students really liked. Kids said that the freedom to choose how to show what they knew and to pick who they wanted to show it to removed much of the fear from the testing process, and that they did learn more when they did additional studying and retesting.

The experts said that they learned the content better because they asked other students to clarify their answers during testing. Standardized, end-of-term traditional tests showed that all students did master and remember the content at a very high level when we used concurrent evaluation. I know that students felt empowered and competent as learners, and I believe that their positive feelings encouraged them to act responsibly during concurrent evaluation.

100

Activity 19

1. The first activity in Chapter 5 described starting a KWL about teamwork. To find out what kids have learned about effective teamwork, use concurrent evaluation. Begin by asking kids to get into the groups of four that produced the group Ks and Ws. (Because members of the group signed the official group copy and the scribe kept the group copy, these teams can reform fairly quickly.) Then say, "Please look over the Ws on the list—these items have been our focus for learning about effective teamwork. Reviewing the Ks and Ws can help you refocus on teamwork and may help you begin a list of learnings. That's the new job. Decide what you have learned about being members of effective teams. Decide what Ws you can check off— what wants have been satisfied. Revise any Ks that seem to be incomplete or inaccurate. Decide what you have learned—fill in the Ls."

2. Tell the kids, "When you leave class today, each member of the group will want to have an individual copy of the Ls that you have brainstormed. Each person may also want a copy of the Ks and Ws. Please decide how to accomplish this so that you have your individual information ready to take with you at the end of the group work time."

3. Suggest that they consider organizing what they have learned into the following categories: what they have learned about forming teams (assigning students to teams), building trust once teams have been assigned, targeting and practicing the use of positive social skills, processing content learning and teamwork skills, and accepting individual responsibility for learning and for being an effective team member. Tell them that they will be asked to explain their learning in each of these categories. Give groups at least thirty minutes to look over the original Ks and Ws and begin brainstorming the Ls.

4. At the end of the brainstorming session, say to students, "I want each of you to individually explain or demonstrate to me what you have learned about effective teamwork. I encourage you to use the group Ls as a starting point. You will need to decide how to do the explaining or demonstrating. You may decide that you want to do a graphic, a poem, a song, a role-play, or write an essay. I will want you to be ready to do some face-to-face explaining with me or another member of the class. You

may want to use a copy of the KWL as you explain and demonstrate your learning. Those of you who meet face-to-face with me may become my assistants when we agree that you are an "expert" on effective teamwork. I will ask you to show and explain your learning about *forming* teams; establishing *trust*; targeting and practicing effective use of *social skills*; *processing* content learning, teamwork, and learning strategies; and taking *individual responsibility* for learning.

5. "As you do the face-to-face work with me or with a classmate, we may decide that you want to improve your learning in one or more of these categories. You may do more individual learning and then ask for another face-to-face opportunity."

6. Ask the kids how soon they want to begin the concurrent evaluation process. Ask them to set a completion date by saying, "I want to be able to close the books on this round of concurrent evaluation fairly soon. What's a reasonable target date? Tell me when you think you can be ready to do this?" Set a date and post it in a highly visible place in the room.

7. As the first few students begin to request face-to-face opportunities, ask other students to continue working on getting ready to demonstrate their learning. Students who concurrently evaluate with you and who demonstrate a high level of learning can then begin to help by doing face-to-face check-offs with their classmates.

8. Ask students to complete the following questions in their course journals after you and they agree that they are teamwork experts:

The piece of learning about teamwork that I find most useful or meaningful is _____ .

The piece of learning about teamwork about which I felt the greatest surprise is _____ .

I believe that my best quality as a teammate is _____ .

The teamwork behavior that I want to strengthen is _____ .

To organize my learning for this round of concurrent evaluation I did _____ .

I can improve my organization by doing _____ .

I believe that teamwork is like *(a sport or type of exercise)* because both *(three similarities to complete the metaphor)*. ◆

Sometimes students demonstrated their learning in teams. I liked asking for team production of graphic organizers that gave information in words and pictures, story boards that sequenced or explained information in words and pictures, poems or songs, and "acting out" performances. I believe that we got better, more complete, and more accurate demonstrations of learning when individual students came to class with a rough version of the product and worked in teams to create a final product. Students learned more about the concepts as they discussed them with each other. They also uncovered and corrected most of their individual misunderstandings during these discussions. They remembered the information longer. Students did receive credit for doing an individual rough version of the product, so they did not resent sharing the group grade with someone who came to class unprepared. They appreciated this individual/team-credit approach to group products because it recognized individual differences.

I believe that many assessment tools are available to teachers and students. By choosing an assessment tool that fits the situation, a teacher or student will be able to collect good information about behaviors and learning. This is authentic assessment. Good information gathering leads to authentic evaluation, and quality results from authentic concurrent evaluation, self-evaluation, personal goal setting, and individual planning for reaching goals. As long as the teacher is the sole evaluator in the classroom, students will perceive that grades are prizes to be won and will become defensive when they do not win the rewards that they want. Self- and concurrent evaluation take the fear out of the evaluation process. They contribute to the supportive, including climate that encourages students to produce quality work.

When students self-evaluate, set goals, plan for improvement, and concurrently evaluate with other students or with the teacher, they perceive that learning is the prize to be won and work to increase the quality of their learning. They discover how to behave intelligently, how to improve, and how to take responsibility for their own learning. They learn how to do their own quality driving in all of their classrooms.

(This one is for the reader.) We have reached the end of the book. Please self-evaluate your learning as a reader. I don't expect you to report to me. This is for your own personal information.

1. I believe that my performance as a reader of this book is _____

    because *(learnings you have applied in your own school setting)*.

    because *(learnings you have shared with members of your collegial group)*.

    because *(enhanced personal responsibility for what happens in your own school setting)*.

2. I want to learn more about _____ .

3. Reading this book has been like watching *(a favorite movie)* because both *(three commonalities)*. ◆

Happy driving!

Bibliography

Armstrong, Thomas. 1993. *7 kinds of smart: Discovering and using your natural intelligences.* New York: Plume/Penguin.

———. 1994. *Multiple intelligences in the classroom.* Alexandria, Va.: Association for Supervision and Curriculum Development.

Bellanca, James. 1990. *The cooperative think tank.* Arlington Heights, Ill.: IRI/ SkyLight Training and Publishing, Inc.

Bellanca, James, and R. Fogarty. 1986. *Catch them thinking: A handbook of classroom strategies.* Arlington Heights, Ill.: IRI/SkyLight Training and Publishing, Inc.

———. 1990. *Blueprints for thinking in the cooperative classroom.* Arlington Heights, Ill.: IRI/SkyLight Training and Publishing, Inc.

Bishop, John H. 1992. "Why U. S. Students Need Incentives to Learn." *Educational Leadership* 49 (March):6,15–18.

Blankenstein, Alan M. 1992. "Lessons from Enlightened Corporations." *Educational Leadership* 49 (March):6, 71–75.

Boffey, D. Barnes. 1993. *Reinventing yourself: A control theory approach to becoming the person you want to be.* Chapel Hill, N.C.: New View Publications.

Bonstingl, John Jay. 1992. "The Total Quality Classroom." *Educational Leadership* 49 (March):6, 66–70.

Burke, Kay, ed. 1992. *Authentic assessment: A collection.* Arlington Heights, Ill.: IRI/ SkyLight Training and Publishing, Inc.

———. 1992. *What to do with the kid who: Developing cooperation, self-discipline, and responsibility in the classroom.* Arlington Heights, Ill.: IRI/SkyLight Training and Publishing, Inc.

———. 1994. *The mindful school: How to assess authentic learning.* Arlington Heights, Ill.: IRI/SkyLight Training and Publishing, Inc.

———. 1994. *The mindful school: The portfolio connection.* Arlington Heights, Ill.: IRI/SkyLight Training and Publishing, Inc.

Chapman, Carolyn. 1993. *If the shoe fits: How to develop multiple intelligences in the classroom.* Arlington Heights, Ill.: IRI/SkyLight Training and Publishing, Inc.

Costa, Arthur L. 1991. *The school as a home for the mind.* Arlington Heights, Ill.: IRI/SkyLight Training and Publishing, Inc.

Covey, Stephen R. 1989. *The 7 habits of highly effective people.* New York: Simon & Schuster.

———. 1991. *Principle-centered leadership.* New York: Summit Books.

Crawford, Donna, Richard Badine, and Robert Hoglund. 1994. *The school for quality learning: Managing the school and classroom the Deming way.* Chapel Hill, N.C.: New View Publications.

Deming, W. Edwards. 1988. *Out of the crisis.* Cambridge, Mass.: Massachusetts Institute of Technology.

———. 1993. *The new economics for industry, government, education.* Cambridge, Mass.: Massachusetts Institute of Technology.

Fogarty, Robin, and Jim Bellanca. 1989. *Patterns for thinking—Patterns for transfer.* Arlington Heights, Ill.: IRI/SkyLight Training and Publishing, Inc.

Gardner, Howard. 1983. *Frames of mind: The theory of multiple intelligences.* New York: HarperCollins.

———. 1993. *Multiple intelligences: The theory in practice.* New York: HarperCollins.

Glasser, William, M.D. 1984. *Control theory.* New York: HarperCollins.

———. 1986. *Control theory in the classroom.* New York: HarperCollins.

———. 1992. *The quality school.* New York: HarperCollins.

———. 1993. *The quality school teacher.* New York: HarperCollins.

———. 1994. *The control theory manager.* New York: HarperCollins.

———. 1995. *The quality school training program, bulletin # 24, intelligence and outcomes.* Chatsworth, Ca.: The Institute for CT/RT & QM.

Good, E. Perry. 1987. *In pursuit of happiness.* Chapel Hill, N.C.: New View Publications.

Bibliography

———. 1990. *It's OK to be the boss.* Chapel Hill, N.C.: New View Publications.

Goodlad, John I. 1984. *A place called school.* New York: McGraw Hill.

Goodrich, Heidi. 1996. "Understanding Rubrics." *Educational Leadership* 54 (December):4, 14–17.

Gossen, Diane Chelsom. 1993. *Restitution: Restructuring school discipline.* Chapel Hill, N.C.: New View Publications.

Gossen, Diane, and Judy Anderson. 1995. *Creating the conditions: Leadership for quality schools.* Chapel Hill, N.C.: New View Publications.

Jalongo, Mary R. 1992. "Teachers' Stories: Our Ways of Knowing." *Educational Leadership* 49 (April):7, 68–73.

Johnson, David W., and Roger T. Johnson. 1991. *Teaching children to be peacemakers.* Edina, Minn.: Interaction Book Company.

———. 1995. *Reducing school violence through conflict resolution.* Alexandria, Va.: Association for Supervision and Curriculum Development.

Johnson, David W., Roger T. Johnson, and Edythe Johnson Holubec. 1988. *Advanced cooperative learning.* Edina, Minn.: Interaction Book Company.

———. 1988. *Cooperation in the classroom.* Edina, Minn.: Interaction Book Company.

Kohn, Alfie. 1986. *No contest: The case against competition.* New York: Houghton Mifflin.

———. 1993. *Punished by rewards.* New York: Houghton Mifflin.

———. 1996. *Beyond discipline.* Alexandria, Va.: Association for Supervision and Curriculum Development.

Lazear, David. 1991. *Seven ways of knowing: Teaching for multiple intelligences.* Arlington Heights, Ill.: IRI/SkyLight Training and Publishing, Inc.

———. 1991. *Seven ways of teaching: The artistry of teaching with multiple intelligences.* Arlington Heights, Ill.: IRI/SkyLight Training and Publishing, Inc.

———. 1993. *Seven pathways of learning: Teaching students and parents about multiple intelligences.* Tucson: Zephyr Press.

Linn, Robert L., and Stephen B. Dunbar. 1990. "The Nation's Report Card Goes Home." *Phi Delta Kappan* 72 (October):2, 127–33.

Mamchur, Carolyn. 1990. "But . . . the Curriculum." *Phi Delta Kappan* 71 (April):8, 634–37.

McClanahan, Elaine, and Carolyn Wicks. 1994. *Future force, kids that want to, can, and do!* Glendale, Calif.: Griffin Publishing.

Newmann, Fred M. 1991. "Linking Restructuring to Authentic Student Achievement." *Phi Delta Kappan* 73 (February):6, 458–63.

Packer, Arnold H. 1992. "Taking Action on the SCANS Report." *Educational Leadership* 49 (March):6, 27–31.

Powers, William T. 1973. *Behavior: The control of perception.* Chicago: Aldine Publishing.

Senge, Peter. 1990. *The fifth discipline.* New York: Bantam Books.

Tribus, Myron. 1992. "Quality Management in Education." Unpublished paper.

VanDeWeghe, Richard. 1992. "What Teachers Learn from 'Kid Watching.'" *Educational Leadership* 94 (April):7, 49–52.

Walton, Sherry, and Kathe Taylor. 1996. "How Did You Know the Answer Was Boxcar?" *Educational Leadership* 54 (December):4, 38–40.

Wiggins, Grant. 1989. "Teaching to the (Authentic) Test." *Educational Leadership* 46 (April):7, 41–47.

Williams, R. Bruce. 1993. *More than 50 ways to build team consensus.* Arlington Heights, Ill.: IRI/SkyLight Training and Publishing, Inc.

IRI/SkyLight Training and Publishing, Inc.

Index

Learn from Our Books *and* from Our Authors!

Bring Our Author/Trainers to Your District

At IRI/SkyLight, we have assembled a unique team of outstanding author/trainers with international reputations for quality work. Each has designed high-impact programs that translate powerful new research into successful learning strategies for every student. We design each program to fit your school's or district's special needs.

Training Programs

IRI/SkyLight's training programs extend the renewal process by helping educators move from content-centered to mind-centered classrooms. In our highly interactive workshops, participants learn foundational, research-based information and teaching strategies in an instructional area that they can immediately transfer to the classroom setting. With IRI/SkyLight's specially prepared materials, participants learn how to teach their students to learn for a lifetime.

Network for Systemic Change

Through a partnership with Phi Delta Kappa, IRI/SkyLight offers a Network for site-based systemic change: *The Network of Mindful Schools.* The Network is designed to promote systemic school change as possible and practical when starting with a renewed vision that centers on *what* and *how* each student learns. To help accomplish this goal, Network consultants work with member schools to develop an annual tactical plan and then implement that plan at the classroom level.

Training of Trainers

The Training of Trainers programs train your best teachers, those who provide the highest quality instruction, to coach other teachers. This not only increases the number of teachers you can afford to train in each program, but also increases the amount of coaching and follow-up that each teacher can receive from a resident expert. Our Training of Trainers programs will help you make a systemic improvement in your staff development program.

To receive a FREE COPY of the IRI/SkyLight catalog or more information about trainings offered through IRI/SkyLight, contact CLIENT SERVICES at

TRAINING AND PUBLISHING, INC.
2626 S. Clearbrook Dr., Arlington Heights, IL 60005
800-348-4474 • 847-290-6600 • FAX 847-290-6609

There are
one-story intellects,
two-story intellects, and three-story
intellects with skylights. All fact collectors, who
have no aim beyond their facts, are one-story men. Two-story men
compare, reason, generalize, using the labors of the fact collectors as
well as their own. Three-story men idealize, imagine,
predict—their best illumination comes from
above, through the skylight.
—*Oliver Wendell*
Holmes